IF THIS IS TREASON, I AM GUILTY

The Rev. Dr Allan Aubrey Boesak is one of the leading South African advocates of the declaration of apartheid as a theological heresy.

A graduate of the Free University of Amsterdam, in the Netherlands, he has been Chaplain of the University of the Western Cape since the mid-1970s, and is a former Senior Vice-President of the South African Council of Churches.

In 1982 he was elected President of the World Alliance of Reformed Churches, a position he still holds. He is Moderator of the Dutch Reformed Mission Church in South Africa, and Patron of the United Democratic Front.

Dr Boesak was detained in 1985 and subsequently charged with seeking to overthrow the South African government or to put it in danger, but the charges were dropped and there was no conviction.

Since 1976 he has been minister of a church in Bellville, where he and his family live. He is also the author of several books, including *Black and Reformed: Apartheid, Liberation and the Calvinist Tradition*, *The Finger of God* and *Walking on Thorns: The Call to Christian Obedience*.

D1494400

ALLAN A. BOESAK

If This Is
Treason,
I Am Guilty

Foreword by
Paul Boateng, M.P.

Collins
FOUNT PAPERBACKS

Published in the United States of America by
Wm. B. Eerdmans Publishing Co., Grand Rapids, Michigan
in 1987
First published in Great Britain by Fount Paperbacks,
London in 1988

Made and printed in Great Britain by
William Collins Sons & Co. Ltd, Glasgow

CONTENTS

FOREWORD

Allan Boesak's outstanding contribution to the struggle for freedom and justice in his native South Africa is reflected in this important book. The strength and vision contained within these pages make reading it not only a moving and memorable experience but a valuable aid to the understanding of racism at work in South Africa and the world.

The message of this great preacher and leader is rooted in the Christian faith but universal in its application. Allan Boesak shows us how new insights into Christianity come from the experience of the peoples of South Africa as they stand up against a monstrous evil.

Allan Boesak addresses, as few have done as well in our time, the issue of power and powerlessness. The "powers and the principalities" are challenged and required to do justice as between peoples, races and classes. The struggle against racism, wherever it is waged, requires strategy not just sentiment. Allan Boesak shows us how this has developed within the context of South Africa. There is hope to be found within this volume, and a vision of a free non-racial, democratic South Africa.

The Bible is the source of Allan Boesak's authority. Racism is a gaping wound in the body of Christ. Apartheid is shown, not simply as an unjust system, but a heresy. The word is seen to be an enabling and empowering instrument for good and for change. *If this is Treason, I am Guilty* spares the reader none of the horror of Apartheid, its banality and absurdity, as well as its terrible cruelty. This book, however, like the people of South Africa, is a source of great joy and inspiration. Their ultimate triumph is not in doubt. The question for the world is how soon, and how many more must die, before we wake up to the need for concerted international action to help put an end to Apartheid.

PAUL BOATENG

House of Commons
December 1987

1

He Made Us All,
but . . .

In August 1982 Allan Boesak addressed the meeting of
the World Alliance of Reformed Churches (WARC) in
Ottawa.

His plea was for the Alliance to address itself very
seriously to the increasing problem of racism in the
world, and particularly in South Africa, the most
blatantly racist country on earth. There the Church is
openly identified with the prejudice and oppression that
exists in society today, and it appears that the white
Dutch Reformed churches have conformed to this role
more than others. Despite the work of the World
Council of Churches (WCC) to change the situation,
there are many black Christians in South Africa who are
desperately uncertain about the stance of their church,
this uncertainty based largely on the fact that the Reformed tradition has been so effectively used to justify
white racism and oppression there. In Allan Boesak's
view, the World Alliance, with a single stance on this
vital issue, based on its own understanding of the Gospel
and the Reformed tradition, could contribute
enormously towards achieving a greater understanding
and awareness of the dangers of racism by assuming a
more active role in the struggle to combat it.

*

The struggle in South Africa is not merely against an evil ideology; it is against a pseudo-religious ideology which was born in and is still being justified out of the bosom of the Reformed churches. The importance of this for the future of the Christian Church in South Africa is enormous, for ultimately, beyond denomination and tradition, the credibility of the Gospel of Jesus Christ is at stake.

Racism is Sin

It is not my intention to join the current debate about the "right" definition of racism. Even while this debate is going on, the oppression of people on the basis of colour, the dehumanization and suffering, the exploitation and rejection continue. The cries of anguish of the rejected children of God are far more articulate, and the suffering and pain far more real, than mere definitions will allow. Yet we need to have a precise idea of what we are talking about.

First of all, racism is an ideology of racial domination that incorporates beliefs in a particular race's cultural and/or inherent biological inferiority. It uses such beliefs to justify and prescribe unequal treatment of that group. In other words, racism is not merely attitudinal, it is structural. It is not merely a vague feeling of racial superiority, it is a system of *domination*, complete with the structures of domination – social, political, and economic. To put it another way: racism excludes groups on the basis of race or colour. It is not only, however, exclusion on the basis of race, but exclusion for the purpose of subjugating or of maintaining subjugation. It is in this light that the current "changes" in South Africa's racial policies must be understood. The government, instead of bringing about fundamental changes that will secure meaningful participation, peace, and well-being for all, is making certain concessions that will do no more than allow a select group of blacks to have limited economic benefits and limited political participation under white control. The overall effect will not be to bring justice to all, but to strengthen white supremacy. In all these matters the Church is called on to be particularly watchful and sensitive, so that we acquire the ability to ask fundamental questions. Racism is an ideology that justifies white supremacy.

Second, racism has not always been with us. It is a fairly recent phenomenon that has become an essential part of a historical process of cultural, economic, political, and psychological domination. It manifests itself in all these areas. It is important to note that racism became essential to what Helmut Gollwitzer has called the "capitalistic revolution": "The revolution of the white, Christian, Protestant peoples that spread all over the world to open the era of slavery, which even today (albeit not in the same form) is not yet ended."[1] I note this to make the point that racism cannot be understood in individual, personal terms only. It must be understood in its historical perspective and in its structural manifestations.

But, third, however important these observations may be, the Christian must say more. Racism is sin. It denies the creatureliness of others. It denies the truth that all human beings are made in the image of

[1]Helmut Gollwitzer, "Zür Schwarzen Theologie," in *Evangelische Theologie*, 34 (January 1974), pp. 43–69.

the Father of Jesus Christ. As a result, it not only denies the unity of all humankind, it also refuses to acknowledge that being in the image of God means having "dominion over the earth". Human beings were created in the image and likeness of God. In the Bible, "image" and "likeness" do not of course allude to any kind of *physical* likeness, but rather describe our unique relation to God. The likeness is not morphological but functional, dynamic.

The whole story of Genesis 1 and 2 is an attempt to give expression to this creaturely relatedness to God. The responsibility that flows from this relationship is "dominion over creation". This has not only to do with the source of this power – God – but also with those with whom we are to share this unique gift: our fellow human beings. At the same time, we are reminded in Genesis 2 that this "dominion" is *service*, that there is an interdependence between human beings and between human beings and creation. To have this dominion is to share this dominion – it is to be truly human. It means to be able to be, to live, in accordance with one's God-given humanity. It means to be able to realize this essential humanity in the social-historical world in which we all have responsibility.

To share in this dominion as a free person created by God enables human beings to become the subject of their humanity, to assume responsibility, to act responsibly and in acting to realize their own being and that of others. All this racism denies. It usurps this power to be truly human for one group only, and it justifies this action by placing the other on a sub-human level, not truly human, or not "equal", or "equal, but. . . ."

Racism is a form of idolatry in which the dominant

group assumes for itself a status higher than the other, and through its political, military, and economic power seeks to play God in the lives of others. The history of white racism is full of examples of this.

Racism has brought dehumanization, undermined black personhood, destroyed the human-beingness of those who are called to be the children of God. It has caused those who are the image of the living God to despise themselves, for they cannot understand why it should be their very blackness that calls forth such hatred, such contempt, such wanton, terrible violence.

Most of all, racism denies the liberating, humanizing, reconciling work of Christ, the Promised One who has taken on human form, thereby reaffirming human worth in the sight of God. Through his life as a human being he has given flesh and blood to the words of the psalmist concerning the life of God's weak and needy people: "From oppression and violence he redeems their life, and precious is their blood in his sight" (Psalm 72:14).

Through his life, death, and resurrection he has reconciled people to God and to themselves, he has broken down the wall of partition and enmity, and so has become our peace (Ephesians 2:14). He has brought us together in the one Lord, one faith, one baptism, one God who is the Father of us all (Ephesians 4:5, 6).

Racism has not only contaminated human society, it has also defiled the body of Christ. And Christians and the Church have provided the moral and theological justification for racism and human degradation.

Apartheid as Pseudo-Gospel

South African society is based on white racism maintained by violence and oppression. Legalized discrimination in all areas is a way of life. Apartheid means that in 1970 whites, only 17.8 per cent of the population, received 71.9 per cent of the national income, while blacks received 19.3 per cent. It means that whites claim 87 per cent of the land while 13 per cent is "allotted" to black people. It means that blacks are denied any meaningful participation in the political decision-making process so that the process of "democracy" here has become a farce. It means a capitalist economic structure for which atrocities like the migrant labour system apparently are necessary, a system that, as South African economist Dr Francis Wilson has pointed out:

> can and does compel old people living amongst their friends and relatives in familiar surroundings, where they have spent their entire working lives, to endure resettlement in some distant place where they feel they have been cast off to die. This system can and does force a man who wants to build a house with his wife and children to live instead for all his working life in "bachelor" barracks, so far away from his loved ones that he sees them only briefly once a year, and his children grow up without his influence, regarding him as a stranger. One may close one's mind to these facts; one may dismiss them as being isolated casualties for the sake of a greater goal; but the harsh reality is that there are hundreds of thousands of people in South Africa who are cruelly affected in this way.[1]

Apartheid means that the most important thing

[1]Francis Wilson, *Migrant Labour in South Africa* (Johannesburg, 1972), p. 189.

about a person is not that he or she is a human being
created in the image of God with inalienable rights,
but it is his or her racial identity. It means that racial
identity determines, with an overwhelming intensity,
everything in a person's life. It means that hundreds of
children must die – not only from hunger and
malnutrition amidst South Africa's plenty, but shot
down by riot police on the streets of our townships.
But why go on? One should not pretend that the
human suffering caused by this system can be
described in words.

All of this is not unique. South Africa is not the only
place in the world where oppression and exploitation
are the daily bread of the poor and the defenceless.
What *is* unique, however, is the role of the churches,
more specifically, the Reformed churches. In a very
important address given in 1980, D. P. Botha showed
conclusively that the present policy of apartheid is
essentially the missionary policy of the white Dutch
Reformed churches. These churches not only provided
a theological justification for this policy but also
worked out, in considerable detail, the policy itself. It
is these churches that from 1932 on sent delegation
upon delegation to the government to get proposals for
racial legislation accepted. It is these churches that
worked hard to devise practical policies of apartheid
that could be implemented by the government, while
at the same time formulating a theological
construction to justify the policy plans. It was these
plans that the churches finally in 1947 presented to the
National Party – which accepted them as a programme
that became a winner at the polls in 1948.[1]

And this policy is "all-embracing, soteriologically

[1] D. P. Botha, "Church and Kingdom in South Africa" (address to
the South African Council of Churches, May 1980).

loaded", complete with a theology to rationalize it. As such is has become a pseudo-gospel, challenging the very authority of the Gospel in the lives of all in South Africa. The white Reformed churches in South Africa have not yet been able to repent, to correct their stand on the basis of a new understanding of the Gospel. In spite of all the open human suffering, the violence necessary to maintain the system, the damage done to the Church of Jesus Christ, apartheid still has their support. Our Reformed churches are divided on the basis of race and colour, a situation that is defended as a truthful expression of the will of God and a true interpretation of the Reformed understanding of the Church.

Within the Reformed family, racism has made it virtually impossible to share with one another that most significant act within the community of the faithful, that natural expression of the unity of the body of Christ, the Lord's Supper. And so white and black Reformed Christians miss the meaning of the sacrament which Calvin so much wanted to impress upon our minds:

> Now, since he has only one body, of which he makes us all partakers, it is necessary that all of us also be made one body by such participation. . . . We shall benefit very much from the sacrament if this thought is impressed and engraved upon our minds: that none of the brethren can be injured, despised, rejected, abused, or in any way offended by us, without at the same time, injuring, despising, and abusing Christ by the wrongs we do; that we cannot disagree with our brethren without at the same time disagreeing with Christ; that we cannot love Christ without loving him in the brethren.[1]

[1]John Calvin, *Institutes of the Christian Religion*, translated by John T. McNeill (Philadelphia, 1960). Book IV, chapter 17, paragraph 38.

The Responsibility of the WARC

The World Alliance of Reformed Churches is a confessional family. The rationale for its existence, the *strength* of its existence, is the uniqueness and significance of the Reformed tradition and its contribution to the witness of the Church of Jesus Christ in the world. It is clear that it has a special responsibility in this particular situation. Since 1976 the crisis in South Africa has taken on frightening proportions. The events of 1980 have underscored this, and the blood of hundreds of children on the ground is a chilling reminder of the sacrifices needed to still the cravings of the Moloch that apartheid has become. Thus black Christians have said:

> We realize that the racial situation in this country has reached a critical stage and that God is calling the Church as a liberating and reconciling community to identify itself with the oppressed and the poor in their struggle for the dignity which is theirs as human persons created in the image of the Triune God.[1]

The WARC has no less than ten member churches in South Africa. The great majority of them form the "oppressed and the poor" the statement talks about. They have a right to know what the Reformed tradition has to say about a situation like theirs. As far as the white member churches are concerned, they have direct responsibility and the power to change the situation fundamentally if they want to. They should be addressed in terms of that responsibility and in terms of the historical development of apartheid as it has been directed by the churches. The WARC should accept the challenge to address the

[1]Statement, op. cit.

meaning of an apartheid that has been undergirded by the Gospel and presented as commensurate with the Reformed tradition.

The WARC should reaffirm that racism is a sin, reaffirm its support for the WCC (World Council of Churches) and encourage those member churches who are also members of the WCC to continue their prayerful support of the WCC programme to combat racism.

With regard to the South African situation, the WARC should accept that it has a special responsibility. It should declare that apartheid, in the words of the 1978 Synod of the [black] Dutch Reformed Mission Church, is "irreconcilable with the Gospel of Jesus Christ". And, if this is true, and if apartheid is also a denial of the Reformed tradition, then apartheid should be declared a heresy that is to the everlasting shame of the Church of Jesus Christ. To accept the Reformed confession is more than a formal acknowledgement of doctrine. Churches who accept the confession thereby commit themselves to show through their daily witness and service that the Gospel has empowered them to live as the people of God. They also commit themselves to accept, in their worship and at the table of the Lord, the brothers and the sisters who accept the same confession. Confessional subscription should lead to concrete manifestation in unity in worship and in working together at the common tasks of the Church.

It is one thing when the rules and laws of unjust and oppressive governments make this difficult or impossible for the Church. But it is quite another thing when churches willingly and purposely reject this unity for reasons of racial prejudice – as the white Reformed churches of South Africa have consistently done.

In South Africa, as I have noted, apartheid is not just a political ideology. Its very existence as a political policy has depended and still depends on the theological justification of certain member churches of the WARC. For Reformed churches, this situation should constitute a *status confessionis*. This means that churches should recognize that apartheid is a heresy, contrary to the Gospel and inconsistent with the Reformed tradition, and consequently reject it as such.

I am not unaware that for the WARC this may become a difficult issue. But this is an issue too long deferred. It would be well to remember the words that Dietrich Bonhoeffer, a fearless partisan in the service of Jesus Christ, spoke to the ecumenical movement in a time not unlike that in South Africa today:

> Not to act and not to take a stand, simply for fear of making a mistake, when others have to make infinitely more difficult decisions every day, seems to me to be almost a contradiction of love. . . . Too late (in our situation) means "never". If the ecumenical movement does not see this now and if there are none who are "violent to take heaven by force" (Matthew 11:12), then the ecumenical movement is no longer the Church, but a useless association for making fine speeches.[1]

Calvin's comment on 1 Corinthians 7:23 takes us to the heart of the matter:

> We have been redeemed by Christ at so great a price as our redemption cost him, so that we should not enslave ourselves to the wicked desires of men – much less be subject to their impiety.[2]

[1]Dietrich Bonhoeffer to Henriod of "Life and Work" in Geneva, 1930s, *Gesammelte Schriften, VI* (Munich, 1974), pp. 350ff.
[2]Calvin, op. cit., Book IV, chapter 20, paragraph 32.

2

Church and Politics

Allan Boesak delivered the following address on 12th
May 1983, upon receiving an honorary degree from
Victoria University and Emmanuel College, Toronto.

*

Political Choices and Deeds

Church and politics is a timely topic. Today more
than ever before, South Africans are thinking about
the relationship between the Church and politics.
Although the witness of the Church in the political
arena in our country is not new, I dare say that never
before has the churches' political responsibility been
so pronounced or elicited such a response from the
powers that be.

In Britain, church/state relations are strained because the Anglican Church refused to provide
theological sanction for Britain's Falklands war and
continues to ask some very critical questions with
regard to its own role as state church in that country.
In the United States, officials of the Reagan
administration fulminate against churches that have
gone "soft" on communism, because of the churches'
criticism of the defence policies of that administration.
In West Germany, the German Democratic Republic,

and the Netherlands, the churches' insistence on nuclear disarmament has caused the same tensions.

In my own country things are coming to a head, as can be seen in the Government Commission of Inquiry into the affairs of the South African Council of Churches (SACC). Some time ago, the South African police submitted to that commission a voluminous and most remarkable report on the SACC, in which the Council is accused of condoning violence and creating a climate for revolution. In regard to the report of the South African police, let me say this: that report reveals more about the South African police and about the government they serve than it does about the South African Council of Churches. Furthermore, the Council is being accused of helping the victims of oppression, of giving legal aid to those charged in political trials, of helping the dependants of those who are banned or imprisoned on Robben Island or detained without trial, of helping black children to get an education. I want to say that we should actually be proud of these accusations. It is not a shame to be the voice of the voiceless and to struggle for justice for all of God's children in this land. It is not a shame to give support (even a few measly rands per month) to the families of those who are in prison. It is not a shame to help those charged under laws which should not have been on the statute books anyhow. It is not a shame when the Church, in its own weakness, seeks to help the weak, the lonely, the dejected, the poor, and the destitute. And inasmuch as the Council has been able to do that vicariously for all the churches, I say: Praise be to God! And I thank Him that He has been able, in spite of our weaknesses, to use the churches in this way.

It is clear that in South Africa the Church is on

trial, and a careful reading of the report submitted by the South African police leaves no doubt about that. But I am absolutely certain in my mind that history will prove that it is not the Church which is on trial, but rather South Africa and its government, and if they are put on the scales of eternal justice, it is they who will be found wanting.

Yet there are other examples: churches in South Africa have taken a clear stand on issues like conscientious objection, the presence of chaplains in the South African Defence Force, the civil war being fought on Namibia's border. There is the stand of the Roman Catholic Church on SWAPO (the South West Africa People's Organization), and the situation in Namibia, and there is the Dutch Reformed Mission Church's declaration that apartheid is a heresy, with all that declaration's political and theological consequences.

So, on a worldwide scale, we find ourselves in the remarkable situation that while the Church in countries like the USA and Britain is accused of not being violent enough, the Church in our country is accused of instigating revolution. In truth, in all these instances the basic problem is the same. The Church refuses to accept uncritically the policies laid down by a specific government. The remedy for these governments in each case seems to be to warn the Church to keep out of politics and to stick to its real business, namely, to preach the Gospel.

But there is more than just a little bit of hypocrisy involved here. President Reagan, for example, while running for office, made use quite unashamedly of large groups of conservative Christians and churches who helped him win the election. Then there was no thought of telling churches and Christians to keep out of politics. Now, however, when churches are resisting his policies and getting the support of many, the admonition returns.

In South Africa the situation is of course no different. One minister of the Church does nothing else but engage in party politics. That creates no problem because he is in agreement with the government. Another minister, who publicly voices the criticism of the Church against government policy, however, is immediately accused of "leaving the pulpit" to "dabble in politics". The point is: as long as the Church agrees with whatever government policy may be, it can be as political as it likes. The moment the Church becomes critical it is driven into the wilderness of esoteric spirituality.

But there is more to be said about this. In the past fifty-odd years radical developments have taken place in the social, economic, and political fields. These changes are of such a nature that the socio-political issues have become increasingly inescapable. We have gained a better understanding of the political reality and its human quality. We have learned that social and political structures are not unalterables given by God, but created by human beings and therefore changeable. In addition we have begun to realize the growing political responsibility of the Church in general and of Christians in particular.

Furthermore, the Church knows that its witness in the world cannot be curtailed by the warning to proclaim the "pure Gospel". For what is pure Gospel? It is surely the good news of the liberation of God in Jesus Christ for all humankind. But this salvation is the salvation of the whole person, not only the "soul" or "inner being". The Jesus Christ preached by the Church became flesh, took on a human body, and came to live among people. His message of liberation is meant for the whole person, for people in all the aspects of their lives and their full human state.

There is another important issue, however. Some people feel that the Church should be silent on controversial issues such as politics, for to speak out means to take sides. This argument forgets that silence can also imply condonation. More particularly, in a situation where there is a constant struggle for justice and human dignity and against structures promoting iniquity, neutrality is not possible. On the contrary, neutrality is the most revolting partisanship there is. It is to take the side of the powerful, of injustice, without accepting responsibility for it. This, it seems to me, is the worst kind of politics and the most reprehensible kind of "Christianity". When the situation is as clear and as unmistakable as it is in South Africa, and when the cry of the poor and miserable rises to God day and night, and the injustice is there for all to see, it is unforgivable for Christians and churches to want to stay "neutral", to want to approach reality in a so-called "dialectic" way, and to find it apparently impossible to arrive unambiguously at the side of right and righteousness.

Church and Politics

Before going any further, we must endeavour to get some clarity about the terms we are using. What do we mean by *the Church*, and what do we mean by *politics*? I hope the unavoidable brevity does not unduly distort. *The Church* is the people of God, those who confess not only their belief that God exists but also that in his Son Jesus Christ they have found new life, new meaning, and indeed have become a new creation. As such the Church, the people of God, are strangers in this world, which means that they recognize that what this world has to offer, the structures of this world, the powers in this world, do not have the last and final binding force on their lives. They believe that there is more to life than what is readily seen and understood in the world.

They live for a kingdom which is not of this world. And yet, the Church is the Church *in* the world, and cannot escape it. It is *in* this world that the Church must witness to God's kingdom and it is *in* this world that signs of God's kingdom must be erected.

Put very simply, *politics* is the ordering, the organization of the political, social, and economic life of people within a state, in order to create and maintain a society which is as meaningful, just, and humane as possible. To that end, a state needs government, laws, agreement among the people, and the consent of the people to be so governed.

Politics is therefore a very human business. It has to do with *people*. It has a profound influence on every aspect of people's lives. It determines to a large extent the presence of justice in society; it determines the measure of peace in the world; it determines the measure of human-beingness of people in a particular society. Because this is so, and because politics has to do with people who are created in the image of God – people for whom He has in mind a life full of meaning, abundance, joy; people for whom Jesus Christ has given his life – therefore politics is also, very much so, the business of the Church.

The political responsibility of the Church is to witness to God's demands for justice and peace, for a meaningful life for His people in the world. The vision of the prophet Isaiah is both God's demand for the present and an anticipation of what shall ultimately be reality in spite of the powers of the world who resist it. And it is a profoundly *political* vision:

> There shall not be an infant that dies untimely . . . [my people] shall build houses and live in them, they will plant vineyards and eat their fruit. They will not build houses for others to live in, or plant and not eat the fruit. . . . Their labour shall not be in vain and the lives of their children shall not be destroyed. . . . (Isaiah 65:20–24)

So for the Church, politics is not only a reflection of what is but also a continuous struggle for what ought to be. Or to put it differently: politics is not only the art of the possible; for the Christian it is the expression of our belief that we expect the coming of the Lord.

In carrying out its political responsibility, the Church is guided by the Word of God. This Word is the Word that gives life, and it cannot at the same time be the justification of that death which comes through oppression and inhumanity. It is the Word that speaks to our total human condition and offers salvation that is total and complete.

For us today this means that although the Bible is not a handbook for economics and politics, it none the less reveals all we need to know about God's will for the whole existence of human beings, including their spiritual, political, economic, or social well-being. The Church believes that the Bible provides us with the fundamental principles of love, justice, and peace which we, in the making of our societies, ignore only at our peril. It is the Word of God which is the critique of all human actions and which holds before us the norms of the kingdom of God.

But there is another reality which reveals the inevitability of the Church's involvement in politics, and that is the confession of the Lordship of Jesus Christ. Jesus Christ is Lord of *all* life, even in those areas where sinful and self-willed people will not recognize his Lordship. I believe with all my heart that there is not the slightest fraction of life that does not fall under the Lordship of Christ. Life is indivisible, as God is indivisible, and in all of life, both personal and public, in politics as in economics, in science and in art, in sport and in liturgy, the Christian seeks to serve the Lordship of Christ.

True piety never means withdrawal from the world. The tradition that I represent, the Reformed tradition, insists that Christians are *responsible* for this world. This tradition can therefore rightly be called a "world-forming" tradition. This means that we believe that this world and this history are given their shape by human beings, and we are therefore able to do things differently. More still: we *must* let the world become different. Carrying out this responsibility is not divorced from our discipleship of Jesus; on the contrary, it is a part of it.

In this fallen world, sinful humanity does not seek the honour of God and the good of the neighbour as a matter of course. It is therefore the task of the Church and the Christian to take an active part in the shaping of structures so that justice will be done to our fellow human beings and the honour of God will be upheld. The Church cannot accept sinful structures as if they come from God and nothing can be done about them. We are called, rather, to challenge human history, to shape, undermine, and change it until it conforms to the norms of the kingdom of God.

If the Church does not concern itself sufficiently with justice, with peace, with love and reconciliation, or, more concretely, with the very poor, the wronged and oppressed, it disobeys the Lord and denies the "good news". The Church must therefore be tested, not only on the scriptural basis of its doctrine, but also on the outcome of its diaconal calling, and most certainly also on the evidence of its socio-political compassion. For the Church is not an end in itself, but a means to be used by God in the world. And the service of the Church to God will be known by its service in and to the world.

Freedom and Partiality

It is clear that the Church has no choice: it has a particular political responsibility. It must speak. Sometimes its utterances will be more pastoral, where it concerns a matter not requiring an immediate decision, or where the general opinions are so diverse that the Church can only gradually guide the people to a decision. Sometimes the Church will have to speak in a prophetic, admonishing way, even judgementally, especially if there is much at stake, even for just *one* person: life or death, freedom or bondage, the integrity of the Church or the credibility of the Gospel. Apartheid is an example of the latter. The Church finds the entire ideology with all its practical implications so much in conflict with the fundamental principles of the Gospel that no other language is permitted here.

This can cause tension within the Church, which will quite rightly have to guard against rashness, and give deliberate polarization no quarter. But it is unrealistic to think that all church members will be satisfied with the Church's work toward changing political, economic, and social power structures. Those who think that a more equitable distribution of wealth will upset their privileges will never be satisfied with fundamental changes. The same applies to political equalization. The Church will have to guard against having the quality of its involvement determined by the members with the greatest influence and status. The Church will, instead, have to apply the criterion of Scripture, namely the test of "the least of the brothers and sisters. . . ."

The Church will also have to treat with care the very admonition to be "careful". We should like, in this context, to call to mind the famous words of the Reverend Kaj Munk, that Christian hero of Denmark who, in the midst of the German occupation of his country in 1943, reminded his fellow clergy that the symbols of the Church had always been the lion, the lamb, the fish, and the dove, but *never* the chameleon. And when the Church was cautioned to be careful in view of the difficulty of the situation (the Germans were merciless, after all, and many members of the Church were sympathetic to the Nazis), Kaj Munk ended an address on "The Calling of the Preacher Today" with the words: "What is our duty, brothers? Shall I say faith, hope, and love? Those are fine words. But I shall rather say: courage. No, that too is not challenging enough to be the *whole* truth. My dear brothers in the service of the Lord, our calling today is: recklessness."

What Kaj Munk speaks of is the dauntlessness to stand up for what is right, the holy wrath against injustice and inhumanity, the refusal to call a lie a truth, and the simple belief that constant obedience leads to liberation.

In our situation the Church must also, with regard to politics, and *especially* with regard to politics, have the kind of courage to say what nobody any longer dares to say.

In saying all this, I must emphasize that the Gospel is free and not to be identified with any party ideology. For this reason the Church should not become servant to any party or any ideological grouping. It must retain its critical distance simply because its loyalty is not to any party or grouping, but ultimately to the Lord and his kingdom.

None the less that same Gospel calls for clear choices. The God of the Bible is a God of such choices. He is called the God of the poor (Psalms 72, 82, 146) because He stands on the side of the poor, the oppressed, and the downtrodden. The Church has no other option but to follow its Lord in this. This means that the Church will have to make concrete political decisions and make clear political choices.

It is possible, therefore, that the Church, while rejecting the policy of a particular political party on a specific issue, may have to support another party whose policy on that specific issue is more in accord with the criteria the Church has to apply. In doing this the Church does not surrender itself to the party – the choice is an *ad hoc* one, for a specific moment and on a specific issue. What is at stake here is not a blanket divine sanction for the party as party, but the legitimacy of a specific, important issue on which this particular party has taken the right stand in the judgement of the Church. This is indeed the sharp edge of the knife and here the Church must move with delicate sensitivity.

Many have said that the churches in South Africa, in taking the clear stand that they have with regard to the government's constitutional proposals, have embroiled themselves in party politics. In terms of our reasoning until now, we must reject that claim. But we must reject it also in terms of this particular issue itself.

The Church, not bound by the ethnic parameters laid down by the government and speaking therefore for its members across the colour lines drawn by the state, finds itself, in its opposition to the government, opposed by an ethnic political party. Does that make the Church's stance a party-political one? The answer must surely be *no*. Moreover, the churches' opposition to these new proposals is consistently in line with the churches' stand on apartheid. The churches are convinced that these new proposals do not represent meaningful change away from apartheid, but rather an entrenchment of apartheid. It gives the system more elasticity which (a) gives the system a longer lease on life; (b) makes meaningful change even more difficult; and (c) exacerbates the already volatile situation in which we find ourselves.

Therefore, the churches are opposing the same basic ideology (albeit with a new multicoloured face) that they have been opposing for so long. To take an example from my own church, the Dutch Reformed Mission Church. Synod decisions from 1978 and 1982 affirm that apartheid is contrary to the Gospel – the 1982 synod speaks of "heresy" and "idolatry". Synod speaks of the demand of the Gospel that "justice be done to all [South Africa's people]". A report to the 1982 synod asks for "meaningful participation in a democratic process of decision making and consultation" and judged it "in accord with the biblical demand for justice". In this process, "no population group shall be excluded. . . ."

But the D. R. (Dutch Reformed) Mission Church went further. It adopted a proposed confession with more than ecclesiastical consequences. This confession not only rejects emphatically the separation of people on ethnic grounds, but also states boldly that the Church ought to be on the side of those who suffer injustice and oppression. The confession says: "We believe that God . . . is in a special way the God of the destitute, the poor and the wronged and that He calls His Church to follow Him in this; . . . that the Church as the possession of God must stand where He stands, namely against injustice and with the wronged; that in following Christ the Church must witness against the powerful and privileged who selfishly seek to control and harm others."

In the new constitutional proposals, the enforced separation of people on ethnic grounds, the exclusion of others from meaningful participation, continue. Clearly, the injustices are being perpetuated. The line of exclusion is not eradicated but simply shifted.

So-called "coloured" and "Indians" are being incorporated into the privileged (white) class "who selfishly seek their own interests and seek to control and harm others", as the confession says. Therefore, the D. R. Mission Church has no option. In terms of its own principled reasoning, its own theological convictions, it has to say "no" to these proposals. And it has indeed done so. I submit that this is not a party-political stand, but a stand based on the understanding of the Church of the demands of the Gospel. We are saying nothing new: we are simply affirming a broad ecumenical consensus.

Of course one may ask if such an explicit attitude

does not jeopardize the unity of the Church, as some have indeed suggested. I think that that is a legitimate concern. But in the Church our concern is not only the *unity within* the Church but also the *truth* without which the Church cannot live. We are concerned not only about the *common mind* of the church but even more about the *faithful obedience* to the Lord of the Church. If the unity of the Church is not built upon the passion for truth, the desire for justice, the faithful obedience to the Lord whatever the cost, then it is no unity at all.

And it is that we are reminded of by the words of Bullinger, the young successor to Ulrich Zwingli in Zurich. The city council, after being disturbed by the political pronunciations of the young preacher, had issued the famous Article Four, which stated that the city should call only ministers who were "men of peace". Furthermore, the city would allow no interference with politics, but "you must leave us to govern . . . in as Christian a fashion as we can, according to what would be advantageous for our country." In response, Bullinger reminded them of the political content of the Bible itself and went on to say, "We do not have the authority to withdraw the Word of God from anything at all in this world."

Oh, for a Church today that would be as forthright, as simple, as clear, as faithful!

In this, as in all matters, it remains true: the Church is the chosen people of God. Many are called, but few are chosen. And the chosen shall be known by their choices.

3

A Christian Response
to the New Constitution

The government proposed a new constitution which called for a three-house parliament, composed of white, "coloured" (mixed race), and Asian (Indian) segments. Allan Boesak delivered this reaction to this proposal in Durban on 21st May 1983.

*

The churches have to remain clear and unambiguous in our opposition to the new constitutional proposals for several reasons. The preamble to these new proposals states that the constitution seeks "to uphold Christian standards" in South Africa. We are led to believe that that assertion is based on the fact that this country wants to be a "Christian" country, and that its government wants to be known as a "Christian" government. That also implies that the government knows and understands the commandments of the God of the Bible in terms of justice, peace, and human liberation, and that what the government does is to govern in such a way that these goals are realized and that the glory of God is served. There is of course the further implication that such a "Christian" government should have the full support of the Christian Church.

But let us first concentrate on what the government considers to be the "Christian standards" it is called to uphold through the implementation of the new proposals. Among these Christian standards, we are told, are:

- the integrity and freedom of the country
- the maintenance of law and order
- an independent judiciary
- private enterprise
- the duty to seek world peace

Apart from the important question of why the government should choose to ignore the pluriform nature of our South African society – after all, how should a good Muslim or a dedicated Hindu co-operate in upholding Christian standards? – there is another question. Should our Christian standards be forced down the throats of those who do not adhere to Christianity? Should we not rather live in such a way that others are attracted to the Church and to the Gospel, not because it will be politically advantageous, but because the witness, the lifestyle, the courage and faithfulness of Christians will be such that others will ask: "Who is this Jesus whom you proclaim?"

But still another question remains, namely, what is "Christian" in what the government is trying to do? Something is not "Christian" simply because a government declares it so. Rather, it is Christian because it is in accord with the demands of the Gospel of Jesus the Messiah. The Christian Church in South Africa must not be intimidated or brainwashed by propaganda in our efforts to discern what is Christian or not. We are called, rather, to test the spirits, and to apply the criteria of the kingdom of God – justice, love, peace, reconciliation – in this process of discernment. And these are the criteria we will apply in judging whether the constitutional proposals are in accord with the Gospel or not.

Let us therefore look at these "Christian aims" in the proposed constitution a little more closely. And in doing so we must look not only at the terminology used but also at the context within which it is used.

*

We must, as Christians, the constitution says, preserve the integrity and freedom of our country. But already here the questions abound. What is freedom? And who is free in South Africa – in other words, whose freedom must be defended? In what lies the integrity of our country? Does it not lie in the freedom of all its children, in the diligent pursuit of justice, in the recognition and faithful defence of the human dignity of all? Does it not lie in the fact that the practices and policies of the government are commensurate with the lofty ideals that it claims? Does a land have integrity when it destroys, systematically and by design, the human dignity of its citizens, when it makes as irrelevant and fickle a thing as racial identity the key to the understanding of human relationships, political participation, and economic justice? Does it have integrity when in the name of Christianity it pursues policies which cause little children to die of hunger and malnutrition, which break up black family life, and which spell out a continuous hopeless death of millions of black people?

The vast majority of South Africa's people are *not* free – that is true. But neither are the whites, who think that their security and peace lie in the perpetuation of intimidation, dehumanization, and violence. They will never be free as long as they have to kill our children in order to safeguard their over-privileged positions. They will never be free as long as they have to lie awake at night worrying whether a black government will one day do the same to them as they are doing to us, when white power will have come to its inevitable end.

One has to presume that the country's integrity and freedom has to be defended against "the communists". We have no reason to laud the communists, but we must not blame them for things they did not do. It was not the communists who took away our land, who created the homelands, who drafted the security legislation, who detain those who struggle for justice without trial, torturing them in the jails and banning them into virtual nonexistence. It is not the communists who have created the Group Areas Act and have therefore legally robbed millions of people of their homes. It is not the communists who have killed Steve Biko and Saul Mkhize. So while the communists have a lot to answer for, these things that have happened in this country they did not do. These are done by the South African government, which claims to be Christian and which wants us to accept the new constitution because it claims that it is a "Christian" constitution. No, whatever the communists have done, and God knows their misdeeds are many, they have not done them in the name of our Lord and Saviour Jesus Christ. Therefore God's judgement shall be harsher on this government because it, knowing the Name above all names, has deliberately and consistently profaned it. Therefore the churches, as deliberately and consistently, must remind the government: "You shall not take the name of the Lord your God in vain!" And "You shall reap what you sow!"

And what shall we say about law and order as a Christian aim? Does the government mean the racist laws that have become the hallmark of this country? The Group Areas Act, or the Pass Laws, the Mixed Marriages Act, or any of the other discriminatory laws which are designed to secure white people's whiteness and their privileged position? Does the constitution speak about the so-called security laws, maybe? Is detention without trial, unexplained deaths in detention, and torture a Christian form of law and order? Is Christian law and order the killing of children on the streets who protest apartheid and its evils? No. A thousand times No! The Church cannot accept that. We must be clear in our witness that this kind of law and order is in fact a travesty of justice. The people are not there for the law, but the law, like the Sabbath, is there for the sake of people. Law and order are not the foundation of justice, but justice is the foundation of the law. Order is not the guardian of humanness, but humanness is the guarantee of order. Any order which is devoid of justice opens the door to tyranny and becomes the instigator of the chaos and disorder it pretends to prevent.

The constitution makes the glib identification of Christianity with capitalism. Is capitalism, with its overriding concern for profits and only profits, Christian? Is not God's economy an economy where people matter more than money and profits? Does not the Bible have explicit and disturbing things to say about wealth and about the rich? Over against the self-seeking, self-centred, selfish, grab-ethic of capitalism, does not the Gospel call us to share what we have, not to make us feel good, but in order to create equality among people? (2 Corinthians 8:15). Does not the biblical ethic demand love for our neighbour, so that we first seek the interest of the neighbour instead of our own (Philippians 2:4)? Over against the capitalist theory that the rich must get richer, so that the riches may "trickle down" to the poor, stand the flaming words of the prophet Amos, who did not believe that justice should "trickle down" but rather that "justice [should] roll down like waters, and righteousness like an ever-flowing stream".

Finally the constitution talks about the duty of the government and the people of South Africa to seek world peace. This is a lofty ideal, and I wish that it were true. But to begin with, we will have to state that one cannot seek peace in the world when one is the destroyer of peace at home. It seems that it is forever necessary to repeat the well-known biblical truth: peace is not simply the absence of war, it is the active presence of justice. Peace is the *shalom* of God for the world and for the people of His heart. It is the essence of the well-being of the community, and as such it encompasses *all* areas of life. *Shalom* is there also as a socio-political reality; as the gift of God which transcends any human ideas of success, it is a reality that goes beyond the purely personal and includes the totality of our human existence.

Moreover, in the Bible peace is always closely associated with *sedaqah* – justice –, with which it shall join hands, according to Psalm 85:10; and according to Isaiah 32:17 peace is the child of justice. So in the Bible, peace has to do with human fulfilment, with liberation, with a meaningful life and well-being, and with the active presence of justice.

Again our question is: How can you create peace in the world when you create peace-lessness at home? The injustice of apartheid is an undeniable negation of the peace that the government is trying to seek. Apartheid, with its wanton violence, its destruction of human-beingness, its obscene overturning of human values, is the exact opposite of peace. South Africa's policies are a threat to world peace, and certainly to the peace in this region, rather than a contribution to peace.

The essence of apartheid is the separation of people in society as well as in the Church. The essence of the Gospel is the truth that comes to us out of the mouth of Paul: "Jesus Christ is our peace, he who has made the two one, and has broken down the wall of enmity that has separated them."

In our situation the Church must not succumb to the temptation of the false prophets who shout "Peace! Peace!" where there is no peace. As long as the false god of racial superiority rules this nation; as long as the lives of black people count for nothing and our children have to grow up with hopelessness and despair, as long as justice continues to stumble openly on the streets of this tragic, beautiful land; as long as black and white people cannot learn to live together as brothers and sisters, there shall be no peace.

Over against the deliberate lie that apartheid can create peace must stand the sober warning of Jesus Christ, once spoken to Jerusalem and sadly true of South Africa: "If you only knew the things that make for peace!"

*

I know about the many questions of many of us, the burning uncertainties, the understandable desire at least to know where we are going. We long for some certainty as we face the future. But the way of liberation is never a way of certainties. There is not really a blueprint. It was not true when God liberated Israel from bondage in Egypt, it is not true today. In truth, the only certainty Israel had in those days was its experience in Egypt, as is vividly recounted in the fourteenth chapter of Exodus. There Israel is caught between the advancing armies of Egypt and the sea – between the devil and the deep blue sea.

The people of Israel become desperately afraid, and in their fear long for the certainties of their life in Egypt. For there is a deadly kind of certainty in enslavement: we know the oppressor so well that we become used to a rhythm. In the process of liberation, however, there seem to be only risk and uncertainty. Besides, the power of the Pharaoh was much more concrete and tangible than the promise of God – which was all that they had, really. For, what did they have? – a promise they had not heard (only Moses had heard it), a bush they had not seen as it burned (only Moses had seen it), a land of promise which not even Moses had seen, a wilderness to go through that they did not know, and a leader whose stuttering explanations they did not trust. What was much more tangible were the fleshpots of Egypt (surely a wild exaggeration in the moment of dire distress), and the power of Egypt as represented in the king and his armies. So they shouted their anger at Moses and his God.

And poor Moses? He tries to comfort the people by promising them God's help: "The Lord will fight for you, and you must be still." But to Moses' surprise (and our own) Yahweh gets a little impatient with this comforting, pious theology. "What is the meaning of all this clamour?" Yahweh asks. "Tell the children of Israel to march." Where to? Into the sea of course, and beyond the sea into the wilderness. How? Simply with faith in the promises of this God who has taken hold of this people, who has tied their future to His own, and who will liberate those to whom He has given His heart.

No, there is still no blueprint, there is still no military strategy, there is still no certainty – there is only the promise. *And it is the people of Israel who must take up the responsibility themselves and who must march.* In faith, in trust, and in the knowledge that He is with them, determined to glorify His own name over against the might and pride of the Pharaoh.

I remind you of this story because it is so appropriate for us as we face the choices ahead of us. Behind us are the armies of the Pharaoh. In front of us the sea and the wilderness: that dark and uncertain future of which we know nothing. And the questions multiply. What if a black government is as bad as this white government? How do we *know* things will be different? If only we had some certainty!

But the choice is clear: we are called either to go with this God, on foot, into the sea and the wilderness, trusting only in His promises and willing to do what is right and just, or we climb onto the chariots of Pharaoh. And as with Israel, God will not make the decision for us, nor can we hope to hide behind the pious theological statements we make so often. The choice is ours, and we must not allow fear of the uncertain future to prevent us from doing what is right.

The future does not fall unexpectedly upon us, nor

does it roll in on the wheels of inevitability, but it is shaped by the quality of our efforts in the present. So what South Africa will be depends very much on the kind of foundations we are today laying for that future society.

But this is a false dilemma. The question is not so much what shall we do *one day* if a black government should do something wrong. The question is, what are we doing *right now*, while this white government is doing what it is doing? While it is not wrong to have a legitimate concern for the future, it *is* wrong to use that as an excuse for not being concerned about the plight of those who are the victims of oppression and exploitation right now. And it is a tortuous logic to use fear of the results of oppression as a reason for the continuation of it.

But we have to deal with another and even more dangerous false dilemma, and that is the argument that refusal to co-operate with the government in the new constitutional plan is participation in bloody revolution.

This may be a clever political tactic, but it is as empty as it is misleading.

There is general consensus (even from "coloured" supporters of the plan) that the plans are an entrenchment of white political dominance and of apartheid. What does that mean? Apartheid is an exceptionally violent political system. There is, first, the *structural* violence embedded in the laws and the structures of our society. Every law that sanctions discrimination is an act of violence. When human rights are disregarded, when education is not equal, when there is economic exploitation, when a system by design causes deprivation, malnutrition, and hunger, when the law requires the breaking up of family life – this is violence. In fact, any act which erodes human dignity is an act of violence.

But second, there is also the violence needed to maintain the system, to safeguard the privileged position of the dominant group – the police and military violence without which apartheid will not survive for a single minute. We have seen it: at Sharpeville, in Soweto, in Cape Town, and we are seeing it in the ongoing civil war on the borders of Namibia.

Saying "yes" to co-operation with the very government that maintains this violent system, without first fundamentally changing it, is taking responsibility for the continuation of the violence. The choice for violence, therefore, has not been made by those who resist the perpetuation of the system in the hope of working for a better society, but precisely by those who have abandoned the struggle for a better society by strengthening the present one.

So let us stand firm. Let us continue to speak out for what is right. Let us continue to seek ways toward genuine peace for the people of this country, and let us continue to seek ways to break the evil cycle of violence in which we find ourselves. Let us continue to resist apartheid, to say with Ghandi that nonco-operation with evil is as much a moral obligation as is co-operation with good. And let us continue to strive, to build, even now in the midst of the struggle, the foundations for genuine reconciliation between black and white in South Africa.

As you continue your work against so many odds, do not yet weary. As you work in seemingly hopeless situations; as you see the light die in the eyes of those who have watched the pain too long; as you sometimes wonder whether anything at all will ever change the structures of power that so ruthlessly control our destiny in this land, do not lose faith.

Do not forget that every protest against injustice, every prayer for liberation, every act of compassion and love is an affirmation of freedom and a living sign of the kingdom of God.

And if it sometimes seems futile, and the dark clouds of despair threaten to blot out the sun and your hope, remember that we are guided, not by worldly strength and power, but by faith in God who through His Son loves us and through His Spirit nurtures us, and who has given us a vision that should not die: a vision of hope, truth, love, justice, and peace.

4

Jesus Christ,
the Life of the World

This was the superb keynote address delivered by
Allan Boesak in July 1983 at the sixth assembly of the
World Council of Churches in Vancouver.

*

Jesus Christ, the life of the world! These are words
that speak of joy, of meaning, of hope. For some, they
may even speak of triumph and victory. These are
words that have a ring of certainty in them. Yet, in
the uncertain world of suffering, oppression and
death, what do they mean? The realities of the world
in which we live suggest the cold grip of death rather
than the vibrant freedom of life.

Violence, greed, and the demonic distortion of
human values continue to destroy God's world and
His people. Economic exploitation is escalating
rather than abating, and economic injustice is still
the dominant reality in the relationships between
rich and poor countries. Racism is as rampant as ever,
not only in South Africa, but also in other parts of the
world. In its alliances with national security
ideologies, racism has acquired a new cloak of res-
pectability and has become even more pervasive. In
South Africa apartheid and injustice still reign

supreme. Inequality is still sanctified by law, and racial superiority is still justified by theology. Today, with the blatant support of many Western governments, apartheid seems stronger than ever, and the dream of justice and human dignity for South Africa's black people seems more remote than ever.

In our world it is not the joyful, hopeful sound of the word of life that is being heard. No, that word is drowned by the ugly sound of gunfire, by the screams of our children, and by the endless cry of the powerless: "How long, Lord?"

In too many places too many children die of hunger, and too many persons just disappear because they dare to stand up for justice and human rights. Too many are swept away by the tides of war, and too many are tortured in dungeons of death. In too many eyes the years of endless struggle have extinguished the fires of hope and joy, and too many bodies are bowed down by the weight of that peculiarly repugnant death called despair. Too many young persons believe that their youth and their future are already powdered to dust by the threat of nuclear destruction. And even in the face of all this, too many in the Christian Church remain silent. We have not yet understood that every act of inhumanity, every unjust law, every untimely death, every utterance of confidence in weapons of mass destruction, every justification of violence and oppression, is a sacrifice on the altar of the false gods of death; it is a denial of the Lord of life.

No, for millions of people it is true: we are not uplifted by the word of life, we are crushed by the litany of death.

Yet, the Gospel affirms: Jesus Christ is the life of the world (John 6:35, 48; 10:10; 11:25; 14:6; Revelation

1:17, 18, etc.). This means he is the source of life; he is the giver of the sacred gift of life. He intends for us a life filled with abundance, joy and meaning. He is the Messiah in whose eyes our lives are precious.

But this is precisely the problem. Dare we believe this? Can we believe this without making of our faith a narrow, spiritual escapism? Can we avoid the cynicism of "reality"? Can we find a way to live with that painful dilemma: "Lord, I believe; please help my unbelief"? And even more painful: can we accept the reality of hope and the call to battle that lie in this affirmation? In other words, is the joyous affirmation, this confession that Jesus Christ is the life of the world, really meant for the millions who suffer and die, who are oppressed and who live without hope in the world today? While discussing this theme with a group in my congregation, a woman said quietly, almost despairingly: "It seems you have to be white and rich to believe this."

Good News for the Weak

But there are two things we must remember. First, in the gospels this affirmation is never a triumphalistic warcry. It is never a slogan built on might and power. It is a confession in the midst of weakness, suffering and death. It is the quiet, subversive piety that the Christian Church cannot do without. Second, we must be reminded that in the Bible this affirmation is given to people who in their situation *were* the poor, the oppressed and the weak. They were the people who lived on the underside of history. And it is *they* who are called upon to confirm this truth: Jesus Christ is the life of the world.

In the Gospel of John, chapter 4, the story of Jesus and the Samaritan woman is a good illustration of this truth. She is the paradigm *par excellence* of the despised, the weak and the oppressed, just as children are elsewhere in the gospels. She becomes the very example of the dejected of this world. First of all, she is a woman, with all that that means in the society of her day. Notice how John makes a point of stating the disciples' astonishment that Jesus was in discussion with a woman. She is also a Samaritan, and therefore despised and rejected by the Jews. Her religion is considered inferior, and in her own community she is an outcast because of her way of life. This is probably the reason why she goes to that well alone, at a most unusual hour of the day. But it is precisely to her that Jesus speaks of these unfathomable things: the life-giving waters, and the waters of life.

Likewise, the Revelation of John is written to a weak, scattered underground Church, suffering severely under the persecution of a ruthless tyrant. The followers of Jesus had no recourse, no protection under the law, no "connections" in high and powerful places, no political places, no political or economic power. Their lives were cheap. They were completely and utterly surrendered to the mercy of a man who did not know the meaning of the word, whom John could describe only with the telling title: "beast". From a purely human point of view, they had not a chance in the world. There was precious little upon which they could build their hopes for the future. But like the Samaritan woman, *they* are the ones who hear the message and to whom this is proclaimed: "I am the first and the last and the living One." They knew with a certainty not born of earthly power: Jesus Christ, not the Caesar (in spite of all *his* power!), is the life of the world. The imperial claims of divinity, of immortality, of omniscience and power are the lies, the half-truths, the propaganda without which no tyrant can survive. But the truth stands: Jesus Christ is the life of the world, and he is indeed the Lord of life.

The Church understood this confession not only as comfort in times of trial and darkness but also as an essential part of that basic confession: Jesus Christ is Lord. In this way it became not only comfort to the persecuted, oppressed Church but also a ringing protest against the arrogance of earthly potentates who wanted desperately to create the impression that *they* decided over the life and death of the people of God. And the Church knew this confession to be the truth, not only for the life hereafter, but the truth for the very life and the very world in which they struggled to believe, to be faithful, to be obedient. To understand that is to understand the power – nay more, to experience the power – of the life-giving Word. It is to drink of the life-giving and living waters even when one is faced with suffering, destruction and death. It is to understand and experience what it means to worship the living One in Spirit and in truth.

This worship is not confined to certain moments only. This is a worship that encompasses all of our life, so that every prayer for liberation, every act for the sake of human dignity, every commitment in the struggle for true human freedom, every protest against the sinful realities of this world becomes an offering to the living One for the sake of the kingdom.

Jesus says: "The hour comes, and it is now." Here the present and the future coincide. The moment of the hesitant yet faithful response and the moment of the favour of the Lord come together.

This is the source of the acts of sublime courage which sometimes are displayed in the witness and the life of the Christian Church. This is what led to the witness of the Christian Church at the martyrdom of St Polycarp:

> The blessed Polycarp died a martyr's death on the 23rd of February, on the Great Sabbath, the eighth hour. Herod imprisoned him when Phillip of Tralles was the High Priest, and Statius Quartus was the Proconsul, whilst for ever is King our Lord Jesus Christ. His be the glory, honour, majesty, and an everlasting throne from generation to generation. Amen.

And indeed it may seem as if for the moment the dictators of this world, the powerful and the mighty, have full control over this world. Their arrogance seems to have no bounds. Their power seems unchecked. But the Church knows: Jesus Christ is Lord of history, he is Lord of life, and his truth shall have the final word.

In the same way Christians in South Africa are beginning to understand that for us God's moment is brought together with our present reality as we discern that the Church is called to an extraordinarily courageous witness for the sake of the Gospel. So we hear Bishop Desmond Tutu, the General Secretary of the South African Council of Churches, saying to the Minister of Law and Order: "Mr Minister, we must remind you that you are not God. You are just a man. And one day your name will merely be a faint scribble on the pages of history, while the name of Jesus Christ, the Lord of the Church, shall live for ever."

The Christian Church can take this stand, not because it possesses earthly power, nor because it has "control" over the situation. Over against the political, economic and military powers that seek to rule this world, the Church remains weak and in a sense defenceless. But it takes this stand because it refuses to believe that the powers of oppression, death and destruction have the last word. Even while facing these powers, the Church continues to believe that Jesus Christ is Lord and therefore the life of the world. And it is this faith in the living One, this refusal to bow down to the false gods of death, that is the strength of the Church.

This affirmation has another ramification. Jesus Christ is the life of the *world*. His concern is not only for the Church but also for the world. In his life, death and resurrection lies not only the future of the Church, but the future of the world. In the letter to the Ephesians, Paul is persistent in proclaiming Jesus Christ as Lord of the Church and of the cosmos. His being our peace has consequences not only for the Church but also for the world. Therefore the Church must proclaim, clearly and un-equivocally, that Jesus Christ came to give meaningful life to the world, so that all human history, all human activity, can be renewed and liberated from death and destruction.

The life of the world, the destruction of this world, and the future of this world, are therefore the concern of the Church. We have a responsibility for this world for it is God's world. And if this world is threatened by the evils of militarism, materialism, greed, racism, it is very much the concern of the Church. It is the Church that has heard these words: "Today I am giving you a choice between good and evil, between life and death . . . choose life!" And it is the Church that has heard these words: "I have come so that they may have life, and that abundantly." And because we have heard this, and because we confess Jesus Christ as the life of the world, we dare not be silent.

Speaking Out on Peace and Justice

This assembly must speak out. We must confess, humbly but without any hesitation, our faith in Jesus Christ, the life of the world. We must, humbly but without any hesitation, renew our commitment to Jesus Christ, the life of the world. And this faith, this commitment, must be the basis of our action on the issues of peace, justice and human liberation. We must not hesitate to address ourselves to the question of peace and to the possibility of total nuclear destruction. We must be clear: the nuclear arms race, the employment of God-given human talents and possibilities for the creation of more refined weapons of mass destruction, and the call to put our faith in these weapons to secure our peace, is not simply a temporary madness; it is essentially sinful and contrary to the purposes of God for this world and for the people of His heart.

I am not persuaded that the issue of peace is simply one of fashion, a fad that will go away tomorrow. I do not agree with those who believe that this issue is simply one of political and military calculations, so that the Church should withdraw from the debate and let the problems be solved by the politicans and the military strategists. I remain convinced that the issue of peace as it faces us today lies at the very heart of the Gospel.

But there is something else I must say about this. When the World Alliance of Reformed Churches met in Ottawa last August, we spent considerable time discussing a statement on peace. During the debate, a delegate from Africa made a remark that very poignantly raised some of the tensions surrounding this issue in the ecumenical movement today. He said: "In this document, the word 'nuclear' is used a number of times, but I don't ever see the word 'hunger'. In my village, the people will not understand the word 'nuclear', but they know everything about hunger and poverty."

What he was talking about was the concern of many Christians in the Third World that the issue of peace will be separated from the issue of justice, making of "peace" primarily a North Atlantic concern. This should not happen. First of all, because ideologies of militarism and national security are international in character and cause deprivation and the continuation of injustice everywhere, but especially in the so-called Third World countries. But second, and more importantly, in the Bible peace and justice are never separated. Peace is never simply the absence of war; it is the active presence of justice. It has to do with human fulfilment, with liberation, with wholeness, with a meaningful life and well-being not only for individuals, but for the community as a whole. And the prophet Isaiah speaks of peace as the offshoot of justice.

So it may be true that the issues of justice, racism, hunger and poverty are largely unresolved issues in the ecumenical movement. It may be true that these issues present the churches with painful dilemmas, but it cannot be that we will be willing to use the issue of peace to avoid those dilemmas. One cannot use the Gospel to escape the demands of the Gospel. And one cannot use the issue of peace to escape the unresolved issues of injustice, poverty, hunger and racism. If we do this, we will be making of our concern for peace an ideology of oppression that in the end will be used to justify injustice.

Separating Truth from Falsehood

Jesus Christ is the life of the world because he reveals the truth about himself, the Church, humankind and the world. He is the Messiah, the chosen One of God who proclaims the acceptable year of the Lord. In him is the fulfilment of the promises of Yahweh. He is the Servant of the Lord who shall not cease his struggle until justice triumphs on the earth (Isaiah 42:1–3; Matthew 12: 17–21). In him shall the nations place their hope.

Jesus, in his life, death and resurrection, is himself the guarantee of life, peace and human dignity. He is the Messiah who struggles and suffers with his people. And yet, he is the victor. He is king in his suffering, not in spite of it. There is therefore an inseparable link between Pontius Pilate's *"Ecce homo!"* and his "There is your King!" (John 19:4,19). So it is that the book of Revelation speaks of Jesus both as the lamb that was slaughtered and also as the rider on the white horse. The One who died is the One who lives for ever. The suffering servant of the Lord is the ruler of the kings of the earth. The One who was willing to give up his life is Jesus the Messiah, the life of the world.

This is the truth that is revealed to the Church even as we speak the words: Jesus Christ is the life of the world. The Revelation of John reminds us of the victory of the saints. But again, it is not a victory brought about by earthly powers: "They won the victory [over Satan] by the blood of the Lamb, and by the truth they proclaimed, and because they did not love their life unto death" (Revelation 12:11). This truth is the basis upon which the Church stands. It is the essence of the witness of the Church in the world. It is the essence of the confession: Jesus Christ is the life of the world. The Church can say this only if we are willing to give our life for the sake of the world. We can say this only if we are willing to accept that the survival of the Church is secondary to the survival of the world. We can say this only if we truly believe that there are some things so dear, some things so precious, some things so eternally true that they are worth dying for. And the truth that Jesus Christ is the life of the world is worth giving our life for.

The truth that the Messiah reveals is contrary to the lies, the propaganda, the idolatry, the untrustworthiness in the world. His truth is the truth that holds the freedom and the life of the world. And this we are called to proclaim. And so, as the assembled churches of the world, let us affirm this truth, and let us believe:

It is not true that this world and its inhabitants are doomed to die and be lost.
This is true: **For God so loved the world that He gave His only begotten Son, that whosoever believes in him shall not perish, but have everlasting life.**

It is not true that we must accept inhumanity and discrimination, hunger and poverty, death and destruction.
This is true: **I have come that they may have life, and that abundantly.**

It is not true that violence and hatred shall have the last word, and that war and destruction have come to stay for ever.

This is true: **For unto us a child is born, and unto us a Son is given, and the government shall be upon his shoulder, and his name shall be called wonderful counsellor, mighty God, the everlasting Father, the Prince of peace.**

It is not true that we are simply victims of the powers of evil that seek to rule the world.

This is true: **To me is given all authority in heaven and on earth, and lo, I am with you always, even unto the end of the world.**

It is not true that we have to wait for those who are specially gifted, who are the prophets of the Church, before we can do anything.

This is true: **I will pour out my Spirit on all flesh, and your sons and your daughters shall prophesy, your young men shall see visions, and your old men shall have dreams.**

It is not true that our dreams for the liberation of humankind, our dreams of justice, of human dignity, of peace, are not meant for this earth and for this history.

This is true: **The hour comes, and it is now, that true worshippers shall worship the Father in spirit and in truth.**

So, let us dream; let us prophesy; let us see visions of love, and peace, and justice. Let us affirm with humility, with joy, with faith, with courage: **Jesus Christ – the life of the world!**

5

God Bless Africa!

We are here to say that the government's constitutional proposals are inadequate and that they do not express the will of the vast majority of South Africa's people. But more than that, we are here to say that what we are working for is one, undivided South Africa that shall belong to all of its people, an open democracy from which no single South African shall be excluded, a society in which the human dignity of all its people shall be respected. We are here to say that there are rights that are neither conferred by nor derived from the state. You have to go back beyond the dim mist of eternity to understand their origin; they are God-given. And so we are here not to beg for those rights, we are here to claim them.

*

Thus began Allan Boesak's address on 20th August 1983 at the inaugural meeting in Cape Town of the United Democratic Front, a party formed to bring together a wide variety of groups opposed to apartheid.

*

In a sense, the formation of the United Democratic Front both highlights and symbolizes the crisis

apartheid and its supporters have created for themselves. After a history of some 331 years of slavery,
racial discrimination, dehumanization and economic
exploitation, what they expected were acceptance of
the status quo, docility and subservience. Instead
they are finding a people refusing to accept racial
injustice, and ready to face the challenge of the
moment.

After more than three decades of apartheid, they
expected humble submission to the harsh rule of
totalitarianism and racial supremacy. Instead they
find a people ready at every level of society to fight
this evil system.

After more than twenty years of apartheid-education
they expected to see totally brainwashed, perfect
little *hotnotjies* and *kaffertjies* who knew their place
in the world. Instead they find a politically conscious
generation of young people determined to struggle for
a better future.

After the draconian measures of the 1960s and the
ever harsher oppression of the so-called security laws,
they expected a people immobilized by the
tranquillizing drugs of apathy and fear. Instead they
find a rising tide of political and human con-
sciousness that has swept away complacency and
shaken South Africa to its very foundations.

After the tragic happenings of the 1970s – the
banning of our organizations and so many of those
who struggle for justice; the torture and death of so
many in detention; the merciless killing of our
children on the streets of the nation – they expected
surrender. Instead, here we are at this historic
occasion telling South Africa and the world: we are
struggling for our human dignity and for the future of
our children – we shall never give up!

In all of this, those in power in this country have made the fundamental mistake of all totalitarian regimes who do not depend on the loyalty of the people but on the power of the gun: they have not reckoned with the determination of a people to be free. Because they depend on propaganda, deceit and coercion, they have forgotten that no lie can live for ever and that the fear of the gun is always overcome by the longing for freedom. They have forgotten that it is true you can kill the body, but you cannot kill the spirit and the determination of a people.

The most immediate reason for our coming together here today is the continuation of the government's apartheid policies as seen in the constitutional proposals. In recent weeks some people have asked me with greater urgency than before (and I am sure this question has been put to you also), "Why do you not see the positive side of apartheid?"

Now when you are white and your children's education is guaranteed and paid for by the state; when your job is secure and blacks are prevented from being too much competition; when your home has never been taken away and your citizenship of the country of your birth is not in danger; when your children don't have to die of hunger and malnutrition; and when your over-privileged position is guaranteed by security laws and the best equipped army on the continent, then I can understand why some people believe that apartheid has its positive side.

But for those of us who are black and who suffer under this system there is no positive side. How can we see something positive in a system which is built on oppression, injustice and exploitation? What is positive about a system which destroys, systematically and by design, the human dignity of people, which makes as irrelevant and unimportant a thing as skin colour the basis of society and the key to the understanding of human relationships, political participation, and economic justice? How can apartheid be positive when in the name of Christianity it spawns policies which cause little children to die of hunger and malnutrition, which break up black family life, and which spell out a continuous, hopeless death for millions of black people?

How can apartheid be positive when it keeps part of South Africa's children manacled in the chains of unfreedom and the other part in the chains of fear? The time has come for white people to realize that their destiny is inextricably bound with our destiny and that they shall never be free until we are free. I am so happy that so many of our white brothers and sisters are saying this by their presence here today.

It is true: people who think that their security and peace lie in the perpetuation of intimidation, dehumanization and violence, are *not* free. They will never be free as long as they have to kill our children in order to safeguard their over-privileged positions. They will never be free as long as they have to lie awake at night worrying about whether a black government will one day do the same to them as they are doing to us, when white power will have come to its inevitable end.

But we must also ask the question: what is positive about the government's constitutional proposals? In order that there should be no misunderstanding, let me as clearly and briefly as possible repeat the reasons why we reject these proposals.

— Racism, so embedded in South African society, is

once again written into the constitution. All over the world, people are beginning to recognize that racism is politically untenable, sociologically unsound, and morally unacceptable. But in this country, the doctrine of racial supremacy, although condemned by most churches in South Africa as heresy and idolatry, is once again enshrined in the constitution as the basis upon which to build the further development of our society and the nurturing of human relationships.

– All the basic laws, those laws which are the very pillars of apartheid, indeed, those laws without which the system cannot survive – mixed marriages, group areas, racial classification, separate and unequal education, to name but a few – remain untouched and unchanged.

– The homelands policy, which is surely the most immoral and objectionable aspect of the apartheid policies of the government, forms the basis for the wilful exclusion of 80 per cent of our nation from the new political deal. Indeed, in the words of the proposals made by the president's council, the homelands policy is to be regarded as "irreversible". So our African brothers and sisters will be driven even further into the wilderness of homeland politics; millions will have to find their political rights in the sham independence of those bush republics; millions more will continue to lose their South African citizenship; and millions more will be forcibly removed from their homes into resettlement camps.

– Clearly the oppression will continue, the brutal breakup of black family life will not end. The apartheid line is not at all abolished; it is simply shifted so as to include those so-called coloureds and Indians who are willing to co-operate with the government.

– Not only is the present system of apartheid given more elasticity, making fundamental change even harder than before, but in the new proposals the dream of democracy to which we strive is still further eroded.

– So, while the proposals may mean something for those middle-class blacks who think that the improvement of their own economic position is the highest good, it will not bring any significant changes to the lives of those who have no rights at all, who must languish in the poverty and utter destitution of the homelands, and who are forbidden by law to live together as families in what is called "white South Africa".

It cannot be repeated often enough that all South Africans who love this country and who care for its future, black and white, Jew and Gentile, Christian and Muslim, have no option but to reject these proposals.

Apartheid is a cancer in the body politic of the world, a scourge on our society, and an everlasting shame to the Church of Jesus Christ in the world and in this country. It exists only because of economic greed, cultural chauvinism, and political oppression, maintained by both systemic and physical violence and a false sense of racial superiority. And therefore we must resist it. We must resist it because it is in fundamental opposition to the noble principles of our Judeo–Christian heritage, and of the Muslim faith. We must resist it because it is a fundamental denial of all that is worthwhile and human in our society. It is in opposition to the will of God for this country. We must resist it because in its claim to be Christian apartheid is a blasphemy, idolatry and a heresy.

To be sure, the new proposals will make apartheid

less blatant in some ways. It will be modernized and streamlined, and in its new multicoloured cloak it will be less conspicuous and less offensive to some. None the less, it will still be there. And we must remember, apartheid is a thoroughly evil system. As such is cannot be modified, modernized, or streamlined; it has to be irrevocably eradicated. And we must continue to struggle until that glorious day shall dawn when apartheid will exist no more.

And so, to those who ask *why* we are not satisfied and *when* we shall be satisfied, we must say in clear, patient terms: we shall not be satisfied as long as injustice reigns supreme on the throne of our land. We shall not be satisfied as long as those who rule us are not inspired by justice but dictated to by fear, greed and racialism. We shall not be satisfied until South Africa is once again one, undivided country, a land where there shall be meaningful participation in a democratic process of government for all our people.

We shall not be satisfied until the wealth and riches of this country are shared by all. We shall not be satisfied until justice rolls down like waters and righteousness like a mighty stream.

*

We must turn to one other important question, namely that of whites and blacks working together. This has been mentioned as a reason why the United Democratic Front has been so severely attacked by some people and why they have refused to give their co-operation.

They are saying to us that white people cannot play a meaningful role in the struggle for justice in this country because they are always, by definition, the oppressor, because the oppression of our people wears a white face: because the laws are made by a white government; because we are suffering so much under a system created and maintained by white people – because of all these reasons, they say there can be no co-operation between white and black until all of this is changed.

I do understand this way of thinking. We have seen with our own eyes the brutalization of our people at the hands of whites. We have seen police brutality. We have experienced the viciousness and the violence of apartheid. We have been trampled on for so long; we have been dehumanized for so long. But it is not true that apartheid has the support of all white people. There are those who have struggled with us, who have gone to jail, who have been tortured and banned. There are those who have died in the struggle for justice. And we must not allow our anger for apartheid to become the basis for a blind hatred for *all* white people. Let us not build our struggle upon hatred, bitterness and a desire for revenge. Let us even now seek to lay the foundation for reconciliation between white and black in this country by working together, praying together, struggling together for justice.

No, the nature and the quality of our struggle for liberation cannot be determined by the colour of one's skin, but rather by the quality of one's commitment to justice, peace and human liberation. And in the final analysis, judgement will be given, not in terms of whiteness or blackness, whatever the ideological content of those words may be today, but in terms of the persistent faithfulness we are called to in this struggle.

Besides, the very fact that we are talking about the

constitutional proposals already reveals the paradox in this argument. The government has been pushing ahead with these proposals precisely because they have been supported and accepted by some people from the black community who think that the short-term economic gains and the semblance of political power are more important than the total liberation of all South Africa's people. So our struggle is not only against the white government and their plans, but also against those in the black community who through their collaboration seek to give credibility to these plans.

But there is something more: South Africa belongs to all its people. That is a basic truth we must cling to tenaciously for now and for the future. This country is our country, and its future is not safe in the hands of people who – white or black – despise democracy and trample on the rights of the people. Its future is not safe in the hands of people – white or black – who depend upon economic exploitation and human degradation to build their empires. Its future is not safe in the hands of people – white or black – who need the flimsy and deceitful cloak of ethnic superiority to cover the nakedness of their racialism. Its future is not safe in the hands of people – white or black – who seek to secure their unjustly required privileged positions by violent repression of the weak, the exploited, and the needy. Its future is not safe in the hands of people – white or black – who put their faith simply in the madness of growing militarism. So for the sake of our country and our children, whether *you* be white or black, resist those people, whether *they* be white or black.

So let us not be fearful of those who sit in the seats of power, their lips dripping with the words of interposition and nullification. Let us not be intimidated by those who so arrogantly, so frighteningly, echo their master's voice.

We are doing what we are doing not because we are white or black, we are doing what we are doing *because it is right*. And we shall continue to do so until justice and peace embrace and South Africa becomes the nation it is meant to be.

*

In the meantime let me remind you of three little words, words that express so eloquently our seriousness in this struggle. You don't have to have a vast vocabulary to understand them. You don't need a philosophical bent to grasp them – they are just three little words. The first word is the word *ALL*. We want *all* of our rights. Not just some rights, not just a few token handouts the government sees fit to give – we want all our rights. And we want *all* of South Africa's people to have their rights. Not just a selected few, not just "coloureds" or "Indians" after they have been made honorary whites. We want the rights of all South Africans, including those whose citizenship has already been stripped away by this government.

The second word is the word *HERE*. We want all of our rights *here*, in a united, undivided South Africa. We do not want them in impoverished homelands, we don't want them in our separate little group areas. We want them here in this land, which one day we shall once again call our own.

The third word is the word *NOW*. We want all of our rights, we want them here, and we want them *now*. We have been waiting so long, we have been struggling so long. We have pleaded, cried, petitioned too long now. We have been jailed, exiled, killed for too long. Now is the time! And as we struggle let us remember that change does not roll in on the wheels of inevitability. It comes through the tireless efforts and hard work of those who are co-workers with God, who are willing to take the risk of fighting for freedom, democracy and human dignity.

As we struggle on let us continue to sing that wonderful hymn of freedom: *Nkosi Sikilel í Afriká.* I know: today we are singing that hymn with tears in our eyes. We are singing it while we are bowed down by the weight of oppression and battered by the winds of injustice. We are singing it while our old people languish in the resettlement camps, and our children are dying of hunger in the homelands. We are singing it now while we suffer under the brutality of apartheid, and while the blood of our children is calling to God from the streets of our nation.

But we must work for the day when we shall sing it when we are free. We shall sing it when our children will no longer be judged by the colour of their skin but by the humanness of their character.

We shall sing it on that day when even here in this country, in Johannesburg and Cape Town, in Port Elizabeth and Durban, the sanctity of marriage and family life shall be respected, and no law shall require of man to put asunder what God has joined together.

We shall sing it on that day when in this rich land no child shall die of hunger and no infant shall die untimely, and our elderly shall close their eyes in peace, and the wrinkled stomachs of our children shall be filled with food, just as their lives shall be filled with meaning.

We shall sing it when here in South Africa white and black will have learned to love one another and work together in building a truly good and beautiful land.

With this faith, we shall yet be able to give justice and peace their rightful place on the throne of our land; with this faith, we shall yet be able to see beyond the darkness of our present into the bright and glittering daylight of our future; with this faith we shall be able to speed up the day when all of South Africa's children will embrace each other and sing with new meaning:

NKOSI SIKILEL Í AFRIKÁ
GOD BLESS AFRICA – GUIDE HER RULERS –
BLESS HER CHILDREN – GIVE HER PEACE!

6

A Holy Rage for Justice

In 1983 Allan Boesak was the first recipient of the Kaj
Munk Award, inaugurated in honour of the Danish
pastor and World War II resistance activist. In 1984
the theological faculty of the University of the
Western Cape, where Boesak was student chaplain,
held a Kaj Munk Week. Boesak delivered this address
on 9th March 1984.

*

A Bookshop in Kampen

"It is better to damage Denmark's relations with
Germany than to damage Denmark's relationship
with Jesus Christ." These words jumped out at me as
I stood in a bookshop in Kampen, the Netherlands,
leafing through a little book with the title *Long Live
Life*. It was a book of translations of sermons and
articles by a man called Kaj Munk, the father of
Danish resistance to Adolf Hitler during the Nazi
period.

I was fascinated by what I read. I had never heard of
Kaj Munk before. I had studied in Holland, in this
same Kampen, a famous old university town, for six
years. In all those years I had not known about Kaj
Munk, what he did, what he stood for, and how he

lived and died. During my years of study, I had heard of Dietrich Bonhoeffer. I had read some of his works and was deeply impressed by this man, his courage and his witness. I knew at once that we in South Africa, with our own struggle against the forces of violence, racialism, and totalitarianism, could learn much from him. But this was 1979. My own role in the struggle for liberation in South Africa as a Christian was just becoming more clearly defined. Only that July I had spoken before the National Conference of the South African Council of Churches, calling for the Church to become meaningfully involved in the struggle for liberation. I had challenged the churches to initiate campaigns for civil disobedience to seek change in South Africa. I had been severely attacked by the government press, and the Minister of Justice publicly warned the churches – and me in particular – to be careful. In response I had written an open letter to the Minister stating my position on these issues.

And here I was reading of a man who was as much involved in the struggle for truth and freedom as was Dietrich Bonhoeffer, and with as much to teach us in South Africa as Bonhoeffer had. Here I was reading his letter to *his* Minister for Church Affairs, written in 1943. The situation was amazingly like ours in South Africa. The instruction given by the Minister was exactly the same given to me by Minister Schlebusch: Ministers of the Gospel should keep out of politics. Kaj Munk's reply sounded with the clarity of a trumpet: "If I, out of fear for human beings, should restrict myself to the role of inactive spectator, it would be a crime inflicted upon my Christian faith, my Danish patriotism, and my solemn oath as a pastor of the Church. It is better to damage Denmark's relations with Germany than to damage Denmark's relationship with Jesus Christ."

I was deeply moved by so much prophetic clarity, so much courage, so much trust in the God of Christ. Here was a man who knew where his allegiance and his obedience lay. Here was a man whose love for truth and for the God of truth had overcome his fear for the ruthless, violent tyrants who ruled Germany and Denmark at the time. Here was a man whose witness is a call upon all in South Africa who love the Lord of justice and peace, an inspiration to all who seek to do His will in our own struggle for liberation and human dignity.

I will never understand why it is that it had taken me so long to discover Kaj Munk. Nor will I understand why he, in contrast to Bonhoeffer, has been so quickly forgotten by the Church ecumenical. It seems to me that Munk has a lot to say to the ecumenical movement in general, and to South African Christians in particular.

A Theological Maverick

One reason why Kaj Munk does not play so prominent a role today may be the unsystematic way in which he did his theology – and the disdain with which he regarded the theology of Europe. He certainly had no respect for historical-critical methods of exegesis: "Even at our little university here in Copenhagen there are still people who, at the expense of our empty national coffers, sit there night and day messing about with St Paul's buts and ifs, an activity which proves beyond doubt how right Paul was when he wrote that the letter kills the spirit."

Systematic theology, he felt, is the "way of the devil to further Christianty". The way New

Testament scholars treated the Bible was like a "crossword puzzle", not much different from "blasphemy". In one of his dramas a pastor says, "I have been trained in theology, which is to say in nonspirituality and nonsense". In a meeting with colleagues he exclaimed: "A minister of the Gospel who remains stuck in the mud of theology will never come to mean anything much to the kingdom of God." I can understand that such open disdain for the theology of which Western Europe had become so proud would not endear Munk to these theologians, whose whole life was this kind of theology. Kaj Munk just would not take them as seriously as they took themselves.

But there may have been something else. Kaj Munk had a simple, direct and very personal relationship with Jesus Christ, and he spoke about it in a way that would often be embarrassing to many, especially those whom one could call "professional theologians". His was a language that did not fit into the scientific mode in which theology is done: "I believe in God the Father, the Creator of heaven and earth. . . . One person taught me that and paid the full price to teach me that. . . . When I was a child, I accepted that on the authority of my mother, but as I grew older, I learned to know a heart that beat more warmly than even that of my mother. . . . That was the heart of Jesus Christ." Such is not the language that gains one entry into the hallowed ranks of what are called "theologians".

A final reason for the relative silence about Munk today, even in Denmark, may be his acceptance of violence as a response to violence brought on by tyranny and oppression. I have a suspicion that Christians in Denmark and in Europe in general may have great difficulty in making a hero of a man who preached revolution, and who called his people to rebellion against Hitler, while Danish churches today are among those who are most preoccupied with the peace issue.

A False Dilemma

I believe this may be a false dilemma. The situations now and then are completely different. During the Second World War, Denmark opted for neutrality and made a nonaggression pact with the Germans. After the occupation of Denmark on 9 April 1940, and the subsequent oppression by the Germans, it became clear that pacts with the devil are as worthless as the paper they are written on. In situations like those, neutrality is criminal, and pacifism becomes less and less an option. In the face of an evil like Nazism, witnessing the continued oppression, indeed the obliteration of the Jews, being drawn relentlessly into the vortex of war, how many choices does one really have? When pacts and promises are no longer honoured, when truth is crucified and the lie reigns supreme upon the throne of the land, when one is not governed, but ruled by a tyrant, how many choices does one have? When the tyrant is so bent on violence, so endlessly arrogant that he cannot respond humanly to suffering, to pleas for mercy, and to the call for justice, how many choices does one have? When there is a war on, and neutrality and passivity in the name of some philosophical principle actually become collaboration with the oppressor while the innocent die: how many choices does one have?

Kaj Munk knew, and those of us who live in

situations like these today know: not many. We understand Kaj Munk as he agonizes over the decision he must make:

> When fire and murder are unleashed upon the people of the earth, it is our task to denounce, in the name of the God of love, everything which we know to be the work of the devil. When the deck is loaded, when cowardice heaps praises upon that which before was recognized as despicable, then it is the task of the Church to realize that the signs of the Church have always been the dove, the lamb, the lion and the fish, but never the chameleon.

Our argument is that in situations like those the choices are often made for us, when the use of violence, as difficult as this may be, is forced upon us by the oppressor. It is then, when options are so agonizingly narrowed down, that those with a sense of justice and with a vision for what should be could find themselves driven to take up arms.

This does not mean that Kaj Munk would naturally have chosen counter-violence. Today, I believe, he would have been with those of us in the peace movement, fighting for the survival of humankind, for the preservation of the earth against the madness of nuclear armament, and therefore for the preservation of our humanity. His love for nature, his fascination with and appreciation of its beauty, his love for humankind, his passion for justice, and above all, Munk's love for God and his humble willingness to listen to the Word of God for every situation in which he found himself – these are, I believe, the reasons why I do not doubt where Munk would have stood today. We should not pin him down on issues and in situations of forty years ago that can in no way be compared with our own.

Munk would not only have done this, he would also have understood fully the situations of many Christians in the Third World who face the same kind of evil oppression today that the Danes saw in Hitler and Nazism. He would have understood the terrible loneliness of making choices, the unbearable tensions between what we believe to be the demands of the Gospel, namely to choose for peace and reconciliation which exclude the use of violence, and on the other hand the grim realization that you are facing an oppressor who does not, cannot, and will not respond to nonviolent pressures for change, to pleas for justice and mercy, and to appeals from the heart of the Gospel.

Should the churches in Western Europe recognize this contribution of Kaj Munk, and should the churches in North America come to know him, and should all these churches really begin to take Munk seriously, I have no doubt that the ecumenical debate on the Programme to Combat Racism would take on a completely different character. It could open the way for a new understanding of Christian solidarity within the ecumenical movement. Munk can become the bridge between Christians from different parts of the world. But only as he is being taken seriously, as his theology becomes real for the churches of Europe, and as the churches in Europe learn again what it means to take the risk of divine obedience.

Divine Obedience and Disobedience

For this is one of the reasons why Munk's example is such an inspiration to me particularly: he understood the risks of faith and he understood the joys of faith.

His struggle was for justice, for freedom, but it was rooted in his faith in the Gospel of Jesus the Messiah. Therefore he understood that it was the joy of faith that led to the struggle for justice; it was the love of God which led to the passion for freedom. It was obedience to God which led to the disobedience to earthly powers who challenge the Word of the Living One. His faith in Jesus Christ, rejoicing in the certainty of the resurrection, knowing that Jesus Christ is indeed the life of the world – that became the basis for his courage:

> Jesus Christ is risen. For that faith I shall fight, against the world, and against myself. . . . On this faith I build my hope, for myself and for humanity.

It was this courage that led him to write his famous letter to the Minister for Church Affairs, in which he addressed the Minister as a Prophet of God and a pastor of the Church. With cool, calm clarity he explained that he would not obey the order to keep out of politics. Instead he would honour the head of the Lutheran Church in Norway, whose arrest (for what the Germans called "political activity") was the direct cause of the circular letter which contained the order. Kaj Munk wrote:

> I have the honour to inform you that I am not only of the opinion that I should not obey [that order] but that I shall act expressly against it. For we as ministers of the Gospel are called to preach the Word [of God] and not to silence it. To accept injustice will have the most dire consequences for our country and for our people.

Munk could have written this to the South African government. At a time when the churches in South

Africa are becoming more involved than ever in the struggle for liberation and justice, and when the black church has become such an important vehicle for the expression of the political and human aspirations of millions of black people in South Africa, the tensions between the Church and the government are fast reaching boiling point.

Many is the time that the government has warned clergy to "stay out of politics"; clergy and other church workers have been detained and tortured, some have been banned, others have been harassed in different ways. The government has instituted a commission of inquiry into the work of the South African Council of Churches, and it is almost certain that the commission will come to the government with harsh recommendations to curtail the work of the Council and to scare the churches into submission and silence. Bishop Desmond Tutu has correctly observed that it is "our Christian faith that is on trial here". For the churches are involved in the political scene in South Africa, not because we want to "play politics", but because the politics of the South African government are unjust and inhuman, they cause discrimination, deprivation and exploitation on a large scale, and they are the cause of the violence which is so endemic to South Africa's apartheid society.

Furthermore, the South African government claims to be a "Christian" government; the people who vote for it call themselves Christians; the abhorrent policies of this government are executed in the name of Jesus Christ. This lie needs to be exposed over and over again. Apartheid needs to be called by its real name: a cancer in the body politic of the world, a shame to the Christian Church in South Africa, and in its claim to be Christian, an idolatry, a heresy and a blasphemy. It is as evil as Nazism. There may be people who find it expedient to ignore the evils of this system or to be silent out of fear of the ruthlessness of the government. The Church in South Africa has no choice but to say with Kaj Munk:

> We stand in the temple of the eternal God. All others have their obligations to this and to that; we alone have our obligations exclusively to the truth.

The truth Kaj Munk speaks about is, I think, the truth that Jesus Christ alone is Lord. He is the Lord of life, and he is the life of the world. This is our joy, this is our strength. It is the truth that makes us believe in him as the liberator God. It is the truth that says to us that God is not honoured by illness, by poverty, dejection and exploitation. God is not honoured by death and destruction, by the inhumanity of apartheid. God is not honoured by the untimely death of little children who suffer hunger while the tables of the rich are sagging under the weight of surplus food. God is not honoured by the naked cynicism of those who seek peace through the terror of the nuclear threat.

No, these are the lies we are called to unmask. We are obliged to tell the truth, to shout it from the rooftops. The truth is that God is honoured when we create peace on earth for *all* people in whom he has placed his favour. He is honoured when the hungry are fed, when the poor and oppressed may taste the sweet fruits of justice. He is honoured when the prisoners are set free, when the exiled may return home in peace and safety. He is honoured when sinners repent and find forgiveness and reconciliation, when the broken-hearted are healed and become whole again, when the lonely and dejected discover communion and closeness with others, and in so doing discover their own human-beingness. God is honoured when we, the people of this world, discover the joy of being the people of his favour. It is this truth which Jesus the Messiah has disclosed to his Church, and it is this truth which the Church is called to proclaim and to which we are exclusively obligated. And in so proclaiming we discover the One who said, "I am the way, the truth, the life". Knowing this is knowing obedience. Knowing this obedience is understanding the call to disobey all who would want to kill or defy this truth.

Where is God?

But let no one think that Munk had a triumphalistic Jesus-is-the-answer theology. Of course, in the end he discovered, like we all do, that Jesus *is* indeed the answer. But not in the simplistic, glib way which has made of this truth the superficial slogan it has become. It is something one discovers only in the depth of pain, in the agony of uncertainty, in the search for hope amid the hopelessness in which faith can bring us. It is despair which arrives as we discover that we don't understand God or what He is doing in the world, the despair in which we find that to appeal against God we have to appeal to God.

We see Munk fleeing his church in Vedersö so that they could call a more believing, better pastor – one who did not feel doubt about himself, his own abilities, and his faith gnawing at his guts day and night. Yet he could not stay away, nor could he escape his calling. The prophet, he wrote, knows that he has been sent by the One who calls himself "I AM WHO I AM" – the One who has overcome him, the One who does not brook resistance. He calls, I must obey.

His faith grew out of that constant battle between him and the God who refused to let go of him. Munk knew him to be the God of Jesus Christ, and yet he knew moments where the tormenting question was uppermost in his mind: where is God? Looking at the world, wrestling with the presence of so much injustice, pain and suffering, he went to court with God, to God.

> The poison gas of the Japanese destroys the Chinese; in Spain little children die miserably; for the last eighteen years the wife of the blacksmith is suffering from an incurable disease; the young couple who were so radiant on their wedding day are now making hell for themselves out of their marriage; young girls play with fire and bury their children while still alive in the dungheap; and in my own heart, purified as it is by the water of baptism, lurks lust, revenge, arrogance and self-destruction. No, we do not understand him. We don't understand why he is silent, why he has not long ago strangled the devil.

These are bitter questions indeed, put as plainly as in the Psalms, to a God who is the same God with whom the prophets wrestled, at whom they shouted, to whom they prayed, in whose response and love they found an answer. Like Jeremiah, who found the answer to his own pain in the truth that "thou hast made me thine" (Jeremiah 15:16), Munk discovers the answer in the love of God:

> The Church stands in the midst of this same world of self-preservation, struggle and sin, showing the way that leads to God. And even if his garment radiates the coldness

of eternity [i.e., the suffering and pain in the world] for those who hide there, they will discover that it is precisely there [in the midst of the suffering] that one feels the beat of the warm, living heart. And this warmth is the warmth of Golgotha's blood.

For Munk it was no esoterical, pie-in-the-sky theology which served as an opiate for a suffering, oppressed people. This answer did not drive him out of the world into an empty religiosity where he became estranged from the world and the problems of the world. On the contrary, this faith led to a new understanding: that God was present in the midst of pain, terror, suffering and threat of death, not to sanction and placate, but to overturn and comfort. It was not a legitimizing presence, but a protesting presence. It was not to say "Be still", but it was to say "Don't accept it!"

When Kaj Munk posed the question "Where is God?" and found the answer in the love of Jesus on the cross of Golgotha, it led him inexorably, inevitably, to that day in October 1943 when he spoke the words which changed his life and the direction of his struggle against Hitler:

When here in our country compatriots are being persecuted simply on the basis of their racial origin, then it is the Christian duty of the Church to call out: This is in opposition to the laws of love and mercy, it is abhorrent to our free, Danish spirit. And the Church may and must go further without permitting anyone to stop her: if this continues, we shall, with God's help, move the people to rebellion.

This was the ultimate consequence of his obedience to God that Kaj Munk was called to in this particular situation.

Towards the end of November I was in a place called Mogopa in the Western Transvaal. We went to pray with the people of that settlement because they were going to be forcibly removed from their homes by the South African government. As I stood there, watching the helplessness of those people who were so vulnerable, so defenceless against this powerful, ruthless government, I asked myself the question, "Where is the God of justice, mercy and love?" As I saw the people breaking down their own homes I was overcome with a nameless and deep despair. Isn't there anything else we could do except pray with these people, assuring them that God is just, that He is love, that He is on their side? As we have been doing all night long? This was also the question put to me by a journalist.

Then I thought about Kaj Munk, and I knew and told him: sometimes there is nothing else the Church can do. Sometimes there is nothing else that the Church *must* do than to pray with the people, to assure them that God is not aloof but present in their situation, in their pain, that He is sharing their pain and despair, that He is with them – not to bless the lie that was happening to them, but to remind them of the truth that is being crushed to earth that it shall rise again. But this is subversive piety, which always leads to the resistance of evil, not because of hatred, but because of the protesting presence of the loving God.

It is the same subversive piety we discover in the Heidelberg Catechism when it asks the question: "What is my only comfort in life and death?" The answer is: "That I, with body and soul, in life and in death, am not my own, but belong to my faithful Saviour Jesus Christ; who with his blood has fully atoned for all my sins, and delivered me from the power of the devil, and so preserves me that without the will of my heavenly Father not a hair can fall from my head; yea, that all things must be subservient to my salvation, wherefore by his Holy Spirit he also assures me of eternal life, and makes me heartily willing and ready, henceforth, to live unto him."

A Holy Rage

In South Africa the words of Kaj Munk, spoken more than forty years ago, remain wondrously, dangerously relevant. The Church is called to seek justice, to seek liberation for the oppressed, to seek reconciliation as her Lord had done.

We are called to participate in the struggle for justice and human dignity. In all of this the minister of the Gospel has a special responsibility. Like Kaj Munk, we live in times when the old answers to important and vexing questions can no longer suffice. Like Kaj Munk, we are forced to ask anew: what is the task of the minister of the Gospel in South Africa today? How shall we face the changing situation? What do we say when, as in Nazi-occupied Denmark, "the lie rages across the face of the earth"? How do we preach when some of our own people, for the sake of material gain and the taste of political power, will sell all that is dear and precious for a mess of apartheid pottage, by joining the government in its new constitutional system? What do we say when it becomes clearer and clearer that the government is bent on using the Church and our message as part of the propaganda to further the lie of the "total onslaught"? When, paradoxically but perfectly understandably, we in the Church who resist apartheid become part of the "total onslaught" ourselves? Again, what is the task and the responsibility of the preacher of South Africa today?

I cannot but answer with the words of Kaj Munk: "For what we as pastors lack is not psychology or literature. We lack a holy rage."

A holy rage. That anger which comes from God – from the knowledge of God and humanity, says Munk. The ability to rage when justice lies prostrate on the streets of our nation. To rage when families are broken up through influx control laws, and mothers with little babies are tear-gassed, threatened with dogs and guns, arrested at three in the morning, and separated from their children as they are being carted off to jail, simply because they are black. To rage when in this rich land children must die of hunger. To rage when old people must be removed by force from ancestral lands, to languish in a slow death in the desolation of a concentration camp called, euphemistically, a "resettlement area". To rage when, at the stroke of a wilful ministerial pen, millions lose their citizenship of the land of their birth. To rage against the inhumanity and violence of apartheid. To cry for the loss of love and future. To rage against the misuse of God's holy Gospel which is the Word of life. To rage against the complacency of a Church that fails to realize that our country shall live only by the truth, and that our fear shall be the death of us all.

> What is therefore the task of the preacher today? Shall I answer: faith, hope, and love? That sounds beautiful. But I would rather say: courage. No, even that is not challenging enough to be the *whole* truth. My dear colleagues, our task today is: recklessness.

And that's the truth. Oh, for Kaj Munk to live again – in South Africa.

7

Between Faith and Despair

Prior to the July 1984 gathering of the Lutheran World Federation in Budapest, there was a pre-assembly gathering of young people at which Allan Boesak participated in a series of Bible studies. This was his second address to them.

*

> When Jesus had finished giving his twelve disciples their instructions, he left that place and went to teach and preach in the neighbouring towns.
> John, who was in prison, heard what Christ was doing, and sent his own disciples to him with a message: "Are you the one who is to come, or are we to expect some other?" Jesus answered, "Go and tell John what you hear and see: the blind recover their sight, the lame walk, the lepers are made clean, the deaf hear, the dead are raised to life, the poor are hearing the good news – and happy is the man who does not find me a stumbling-block."
>
> Matthew 11:1–6

I have talked before about the dream of God for His world. It is a dream which spells out as clearly as possible the actions of God in the world, and how God overturns human history and overturns human life to become involved with Him in His actions in the world. I have talked about the way the dream is threatened because the world is threatened by the dream. But that threat comes from the outside, as it were – evil forces outside who cannot respond to the dream and therefore have to kill the dreamer.

But here I want to deal with something from within that can be just as threatening to the dream and to the reality the dream represents in the world. Doubt and uncertainty have always been part of the lives of those who believe. Many times we suddenly find ourselves asking the question: Is it really worthwhile? Is there something that I can believe in which makes sense? Does my faith make sense in the world?

All of us have had times when we saw too many things happening in the world which we could not explain, too many things which were quite in contradiction to our faith in a God who loves, who cares, and who has compassion for His world.

Life And-Death Struggle With Faith

I am not talking about those intellectual discussions which I know that some of you have from time to time. I am talking about the life-and-death struggle with faith and with God, because we know that even though there are things that we do not understand, we have to struggle with God because there is nothing else for us to do. Faith in God is the only thing we have that makes sense. But here is the problem if you believe in God: it is God that you have to fight with. This happens over and over again in the Bible. I do not think that when those moments come we should deny them.

It is amusing how theologians try to cover up for

John. They try to tell us that he was not really in doubt. No, they say, it was really his disciples who did not undertand what was happening. So John, in order to help his disciples, sent them to Jesus with the question we find in verse two: "Are you the one who is to come, or are we to expect some other?" Therefore the doubt of John was not really doubt, they say; it was simply pastoral concern for his disciples that made him ask that question. He was only trying to get them to discover the truth.

I do not believe that.

Jesus says to John's disciples: Go and tell John what you hear and see! Jesus knew the source of the doubt was not so much the disciples, although they may also have doubted the point. The real doubter was John. And it is common that people in the Bible find themselves in a situation like that.

Elijah, after that exhilarating experience on the top of Mount Carmel, finds himself under a broom tree saying to God? "I wish I could die because all of this is not worth it! Jezebel is going to get me as sure as the sun comes up in the morning."

Jeremiah, my favourite prophet, finds himself in a similar situation. He is suddenly confronted with realities in his life that he had not counted on. He did not bargain for the experiences that he had to go through, and he knows that he cannot struggle with people about that. He has to talk with God, and he says to God, "You have deceived me", as our translation reads. But that is not the word Jeremiah uses. He says, "You have seduced me! And I have allowed myself to be seduced."

This is a heavy word. And he goes on to say to God: "You have become to me like a deceitful brook, waters that I cannot depend upon. When I want to drink of this water, it disappears, it dries up." In his struggle with God he has to find a way out of his doubt and uncertainty. He knows the only way to do it is to grapple with his God, to get hold of God and pull, and not to let go until that moment finds an answer that makes sense.

We find this same doubt also in the Psalms. I say we must learn to deal with it. Christians have a tendency to run away from such feelings, because we believe we ought not to feel this way: we must always be very faithful; we must always believe everything – and if we doubt for one minute, God will somehow get us.

The Need for Anger

We must not be like that. It is as if we do not know how to deal with anger. We do not want to become angry – Christians do not get angry; Christians do not get upset. We may feel a little disturbed sometimes, but we never get angry. And we have to smile all the time. I like to smile, but there are times when we must not run away from legitimate feelings of doubt, uncertainty and anger.

Kaj Munk is a man that I have discovered only late in my life, and I am sorry about that. Kaj Munk was a pastor in the Danish church who, just before and during the war, became a spiritual inspiration to the resistance of the Danish people to Nazi Germany. Eventually, in January 1944, he was taken away by the Getapo and shot in the fields of Jutland. But Kaj Munk said to his colleagues in the Church: "What we need in the Church" – and I am saying the same to you – "is not more literature and psychology. What we need is a holy rage." Kaj Munk is right!

We need to get angry about the things that are wrong in this world. We need to rage about the way the innocent continue to die. We need to rage about the injustices that seem to multiply every day. We need to get angry at the fact that the powerful and the mighty seem to be able to get away with anything, including murder. We need to get angry about the fact that because people have power and might they think they can trample on the lives of God's people who are defenceless. We need to get angry about systems in the world that continue poverty and deprivation for millions of God's children.

One of the problems I have with the Christian Church is that we do not get angry enough. There is not enough rage in us. We must remember that twice in the Bible we read these words, first in Jeremiah and then in the Gospel of Matthew: Rachel mourns over her children and refuses to be comforted. Something of that we must learn to have in our lives. We must learn what it means to mourn, or to rage, or to refuse to be comforted by the cheap words that we so often use.

When something happens, the first thing Christians do is to grab ourselves a Bible text and dish it out to people like cheap medicine in a state-subsidized clinic. We must not do that! We must struggle with the pain, with the anger, and with the doubt that comes with it. I believe that it is out of this struggle with God that the protest against the misery, the suffering and the senseless pain in the world is born.

We must understand John. He answered God's call to preach the Gospel to the world. He was the one who was called by God to testify to the life that had come. He was the messenger that the prophet Micah spoke about, who would go ahead of the Messiah. He saw clearly before anyone else and said it out loud: "Here is the lamb of God who will take away the sins of the world!"

He was the one who had enough guts to preach this Gospel without any compromise. He had the courage to tell the Pharisees: "Do not think that because you are children of Abraham, God will accept you just like that! God has the power to make out of these stones children of Abraham. There is nothing inherently in you that must cause God to be with you on your side. You need to have a conversion. You need to change your life. You need to become again like the very people you despise, namely the poor, the dejected and the despised."

He spoke not only to the Pharisees, but he spoke also to King Herod. He did not simply admonish King Herod because the man lived with his brother's wife. The gospel says clearly that he struggled with this King, that he attacked and admonished him because of all the wrong that Herod was doing. It was because of this that John found himself in prison. I can understand that while he was in prison, knowing that his very life was at stake there and perhaps knowing that he would never leave the prison alive, he sat there thinking: "Must my life come to this? Is this what I have worked for? Is this how the kingdom of God is realized in the world? What does it help now that the Messiah is in the world and I have given all that I have – and still I must die in this fashion?"

A Nameless Sense of Despair

I can understand why he asked Jesus: "Are you the one who is come or are we to expect some other?" If the

Messiah is really in the world, if the kingdom of God is really in the world, if the power of God is really in the world, why then should the faithful suffer? Why then should those who believe in God continue to suffer, while those like Herod, who live in injustice, continue to be in power?

"Are you the one who is come or are we to expect some other?"

This happens so often in the world. In the middle of the 1850s, when slavery in the United States was still a reality, a black bishop, Bishop Nathanael Pole said: "If I were to believe that all this" – the suffering, the pain, the murder of black people in the United States – "was the will of God and that this had His approval, I should deny my faith and throw my Bible into the heart of the sea." I can understand that Bishop.

I have seen this very often in the young people that I work with. I am sure that many of you have had experiences like this: What happens to you when you decide that you will give your life, all of your commitment and all that you have, for the struggle for peace and justice? What happens to you, when you refuse to accept this world as it is, and you decide that there must be a different world?

What happens is that you commit yourself to find that different world. You want that different life. But maybe that commitment breaks up relationships with friends or, even more difficult, it breaks up relationships with parents. I have often had to try to bring parents and children together when their relationship seemed permanently destroyed because of the commitment of the children to things that their parents never understood.

Much doubt rises up in our hearts when we realize that the struggle for justice, peace and humanity has been going on for so long. I know there are young people who think that the struggle really begins when they enter into it. But there are also others who realize that we have been part of this struggle for many centuries now. I am quite overwhelmed with a deep and nameless sense of depair when I think that in my country we have been struggling with racism, inhumanity, hatred and injustice for 332 years now. It seems that the powers of evil get stronger every day; they do not get weaker. The symbols of whatever is wrong in the world seem to be getting clearer every day. By this time I would have thought that black people would have been a little closer to our liberation.

When the Prime Minister of South Africa travels to Europe, Europe is charmed and enchanted by the man. Even the Pope receives him. What is this? The doubt then rises up in the hearts of our people: "Why? How long Lord?" That is their cry.

What Do We Do?

There is also the helplessness that one has to deal with in the face of all that happens in the world. What do we do about the continued destruction of people? What do we do about the continued disdain of the superpowers when it comes to the lives of people in the Pacific, for instance, where nuclear waste is already eating away at everything that they have, including their human dignity? What do we do about the continuing genocide of the Indian people in Guatemala? What do we do about the continuing assistance that is being given by the superpowers to unjust governments in Africa, in Asia, and in Latin

America? What do we do about the untimely death of comrades and young warriors for justice in our struggle?

If you had stood on the streets of Soweto or elsewhere in South Africa in 1976 you would have seen how the police mercilessly shot down children who wanted nothing else but a different society with a future for themselves. You would have seen, as I did then, what happened to those children and to their parents, knowing that the world did not even blink an eye, and that this made no difference to the world's relationship with the South African government. Seeing all this tempts one to ask: "Where in heaven or in God's name is this God that I am supposed to believe in?"

In 1980 when the school children in Cape Town refused to go to school and demonstrated against the apartheid system, the first boy who was shot down by the police was a child by the name of Bernard Fortuin. He was ten years old, and he was sent by his mother to go and fetch his little brother, because the mother feared that the younger boy might get involved in what was happening on the streets. Somehow little Bernard got caught in the crowds, and he was shot down by the police. As he lay there on the street, his mother came running because someone had told her. She pushed her way through the crowd, and finally she was stopped by the barrier of policemen who hit at her with their clubs and their gunbutts. When she spoke to them, she said, "Please, this is my son, let me go to him! I want to be with him!" One policeman said to her the words that appeared, I think, in every newspaper in the world: "Let the bastard die."

When I tried to speak to Mrs Fortuin two days before the funeral, I found myself speechless. I could not say anything at all. I found that my eleven years of theological training had not really equipped me for a moment like that. I was speechless also because I did not know how to deal with the anger and the doubt that were in my own heart about this God who allowed this to happen.

It is in moments like these that the question of John the Baptist becomes *the* question in the hearts of so many people in the world: "Are you the one who is to come or are we to expect some other?" Moments like these cause me to stop a little bit and to ask: is it worth it? Because one does become tired of this struggle. When this happens, too many doubts seem able to stop you dead in your tracks.

There is a poem which expresses so clearly what I sometimes feel, and maybe you do too. It is by a Malaysian poet, and is called "Radiation and the Rubaiyat":

> And yes, I too am
> tired of protest.
> O to be done
> with this madness
> and like Khayyam
> take to the wilderness
> with a loaf of bread
> a flask of wine
> a book of verse
> and a wild wild lass . . .
> But now beneath
> that nuclear
> bough, Omar,
> there's no paradise
> the bread crumbles
> to radio-active pieces

the wine is toxic
the maiden leukemic
a skeleton
screaming, not singing
in a wilderness of ash.

> Cecil Rajenda,
> *Songs for the Unsung* (WCC, 1983)

But still you feel that although you really want to run away, somehow there are things in this world which compel you to continue.

If we turn to Matthew 11 we find that Jesus listens to the disciples of John the Baptist. He sends them a message: "Go and tell John what you hear and see!" Jesus does not enter into some theological discourse on faith. He does not recommend that John read the books of a certain theologian before his head is chopped off. He does not even advise him to pray! He just tells the disciples: "You go and tell John what you hear and see."

In other words, he is pointing to God's actions in the Messiah. He is telling John to understand that something is happening in the world. Something is happening to the lives of people in the world. And whenever one has to deal with doubt, uncertainty and despair, the thing to do is to notice what God is doing in the world, and to become a participant in the actions of God in the world.

What is Happening

The blind see, the lame walk, the dead are raised up, lepers are cleansed, the deaf hear and the poor have the Gospel preached to them.

One of the great difficulties we sometimes have, is simply to see that in the midst of the mayhem and suffering, in the midst of death, and in the midst of so much pain and injustice, there are signs of hope that God places in the world. Our blindness to God's action in the world and to the signs of hope makes it extremely difficult for us to understand what our own action ought to be.

When the blind begin to see, it means that God opens our eyes to see hope, to see possibilities for freedom, to see the action in which God is involved in the world. But it also means that we are to become people who understand that the words of those in power, with might and hatred and violence as their trademark, are not the last words in the world. They cannot really challenge the living One. In the end, the life of Jesus Christ, and therefore our life in Jesus Christ, will be the last word. We have to learn to see that.

When Elisha was fleeing from King Dothan, he found when he woke up in the morning that the King had found out where he was and had sent his whole army to come and capture him. His servant discovered this first and panicked. He ran up to Elisha and said: "Look! Look! There are the armies of the King!" But Elisha saw beyond the armies of the King — he also saw the armies of angels that the Lord had sent to protect him. So he said to his servant: "Do not be afraid, for those who are with us are more than those who are with them." Then he prayed and said: "Lord, open his eyes that he may see."

This is the kind of sight that we need, namely to see beyond Pershings and missiles, beyond might and power, and beyond decisions taken over our heads. God has placed possibilities for freedom, human action, love and justice not beyond, but within our reach – if we will only see. And if we can see these possibilities, maybe we can then become involved in the possibilities to change the world.

The lame walk, Jesus says. Too many times people are paralyzed with fear and depair. We think that we are doomed to sit, that we are too lame to get up and walk. It is possible, Jesus says, if we have faith. We shall be strengthened, our legs will become strong, and we shall walk the path of righteousness and justice.

The dead are raised up. We, coming from Africa, believe that before a person dies physically, that person can die in numerous other ways too. This happens if you have no human relationship with other people, or if your humanity is not recognized, or if there can be no feeling of togetherness with other people, or if you are constantly rejected, or if you have to live outside of human communities, or if the other does not see you.

This is also the meaning of a greeting we have in one of the languages of my country. Normally you would translate it "good morning", but it really means "I see you" – I recognize in you my own humanity, and both of us will affirm that by our relationship. So when we say *"lumela"*, it means "good morning" – but it really means "I see you". Without that living, affirming human relationship, you are dead.

I think that many of us have died because of inhumanity, dehumanization and racism. So many of us have died because we were not accepted as human beings. But it is possible through the power of God that a dead person can be raised up, and we can become alive, and affirm our humanity not only by saying "I am human" but also by acting like a human being who will claim for himself or herself the gifts of God that are due to us.

The lepers are cleansed. I think this means that we are no longer rejected, because we are accepted by God in Christ. Our human dignity cannot be taken away by any document from human hands.

The deaf hear. It is not true that we are doomed to die or that we are helpless or that we have no future. Once our eyes and ears have been opened, we know what it means when we say, "In Christ – the future is now". We may begin to act.

An Invitation to Action

This is an invitation to action. It is an invitation for you to look around you and see what God is doing in the world. It is an invitation to understand that doubt, fear, uncertainty and despair can only be dispelled by our participation, by our believing, and by our actions with God in this world.

There may be very difficult days ahead. In my country there are young white people who have chosen justice and who now have become conscientious objectors. They refuse to go into South Africa's army because they refuse to kill another person for the sake of apartheid. They face going to jail for six years, but they look at me and say, "That's all right, because we know what we are doing".

For many there will be detention without trial, not only in my country, but maybe in yours as well. There may be torture in those jails. You may be banned.

There may even be the ugliness of physical death.

The threat of death sometimes causes great fear in the hearts of many people. I know that, and I have had to struggle with it ever since I became aware of that threat for myself.

I will never forget one day – maybe three years ago – a man came to our door to explain to me that he had been in prayer and fasting for three days, and that God had revealed to him who the real enemies of God were in the country. God had appointed him as my executioner. He was a big man, and all the while I thought, "When is this man going to pull out his gun?" But having given me his warning, he left. As I closed the door, my little boy, who was then three years old, came running up the hallway, and as I held him I realized for the first time in my life what all of this could mean.

I do not mind admitting that it was a very difficult time for me then. I found that when I prayed, I had to pray out loud to make my commitment to God, my commitment not to stop or to falter, but to continue to be able to do what I believed was right. I had to pray out loud because I was afraid that if I did not hear my own voice, I might go back on my commitment.

Through all of this one needs to know, to see, to find the strength to walk, to hear words of hope, to see signs of God's love and action in the world so that one may become a participant.

Let me end with a word of Paul to the Romans which has come to mean so much to so many of us:

"But I am assured that neither life nor death, nor principalities, nor powers, nor height, nor death, nor any creature can separate us from the love of God which is in Jesus Christ, our Lord."

8

I Have Seen A Land

In a highly emotive address at a public meeting of the
United Democratic Front on 26th November 1984,
Allan Boesak spoke of the need for honesty and for
the freedom to speak openly about the problems in
South Africa. He was defending himself against
charges made against him by the Minister for Law
and Order, who accused him of slandering the government and the police force with his reports of their
activities. His argument, as the extracts below so
powerfully indicate, is that only the truth and a
deep-rooted belief in justice and freedom for all will
unite a country so full of violence and prejudice, and
create the land for which so many Christians pray.

*

In Australia I had an interview with a person who
asked me what I thought about what was happening
in South Africa. Among other things, we talked about
the unrest of the last three months; we talked about
the campaign of the United Democratic Front and
other organizations to get people to stay away from
the polls; we talked about the success of all of that;
and we talked about the meaning of what we were
seeing in South Africa. "What does it mean," he
asked me, "when seven thousand troops are asked to
go into – or ordered to go into – the townships?" And I

said that that means we have an undeclared state of civil war.

I thought it was clear and honest, and I thought it was simply saying what I saw was the truth. The Minister [of Law and Order] is upset about that. He is even more upset because I talked about the role of the military and of the South African Defence Force, and I said that we know that they are committing unbelievable atrocities in the townships. I mentioned only one example of that — the example of the little boy who was shot in both legs by a policeman. That story was told to us by the people we visited as a delegation of the South African Council of Churches in Sebokeng in September.

I do not know whether the Minister knows what an atrocity is. I have looked it up. It is, it says, a repellent deed, an inhuman act. Something that offends ordinary human decency. An act that is inexcusable and ought not to be defended. When I hear or when I read of a little boy three years old, who was playing in the yard with his friends and who was shot dead by the police while he was playing in his yard, then I think that that is an atrocity. And if it is true I will say it.

Then I hear that little Thabo Sibeko, six years old, who was sitting on the front stoop of his home, playing with other children, was shot there on his front stoop so that he died as he went into the house, crying for his mother! Six years old! And I ask myself what kind of threat could he have been to any policeman? I think that that is an unbelievable atrocity. It should not have happened. If the Minister does not know that, then he must go into those townships and speak to those people. Or if he does not know it now, I am almost tempted to say then may the day come that he will experience it and know what it means — he will never again say that that is not an atrocity.

It is very clear that either he does not know or he does not want to know what his police are doing in the townships. And if he does not know, and if he does not want to know, he should not be the Minister. He should not be in the government, and in fact not only should he not be the Minister, the government shouldn't be the government at all.

I wonder what you expect when you let the police and the army move into the townships and then you order a blackout on all news. The press is not allowed go to in there; the press is not allowed to monitor the situation, to come and report what they see and what they have experienced. What do you think will happen when there is no possibility for public scrutiny of what the police and the military are doing? What do you imagine is happening when there is no public accountability from the police and from the military for what they are doing in the townships? For when you move against defenceless people, and you move in with full military preparedness, armed to the teeth, what do you think is going to happen when you let these people loose on defenceless civilians and on children, especially when the thing that they have been trained for in the army – the only thing that they have been trained for in the army – is to kill as efficiently as possible? We don't think about that, but when we take a person from civilian life and we make him into a soldier, the one thing that we train him for is to kill efficiently. That is what soldiers do, you know. And when they move into the townships and there is no control or there is no possibility of control, then of course you must prepare yourselves that things will happen that you would not like to happen.

But when those things happen you must not try to make out that the people who talk about it are liars and slanderers of the country. You must rether try to find out whether it is true. This the Minister has not been willing to do. I think that that is wrong, and I think that the South African public and our people have a right to know what is happening in the townships. . . .

There is an all-pervading atmosphere of violence and of threat and of intimidation [in South Africa], so that even those people who have suffered under the violence of the police sometimes are too afraid to come out and testify to it. Apartheid is a violent system; we have said so often before. It is a system that can only be maintained by ongoing violence, by wanton violence. It is a system that would not survive for one single moment if there were no police force or if there were no army, if there were no violent reaction from the government every single time the people protested. In every police state the police and the army are not really instruments at the service of all of the people, because they become the instruments of the most vicious kind of oppression to maintain the position of power of those who see themselves as the powerful group. And this police state is no exception.

This is what we have seen, over the last three months. And when we read these things that have happened to our people, and when you read what happens to people like little Thabo Sibeko, the question for me is not only, "What kind of mentality does a policeman have who will pick up a gun and shoot a six-year-old in the back?", but the question is ultimately and finally, "What kind of climate has been created in a country where such a thing is actually possible – where a policeman can do it and get away with it?" *That* is the question that we have to ask.

And so the responsibility for the violence that we have to live with every day, the responsibility for the violence that is systemic – built into the system of apartheid – the responsibility for making it impossible for people really to work for peace without the threat of death – that responsibility I lay squarely at the door of the South African government. They are responsible and they must be told this, and I will tell them so long as God gives me breath in my body. I recognize that it is the responsibility of the Minister to protect his police force, but I must also say that it is my responsibility to protect my people. And I will not allow these things to happen – when I know about them and I am being told about them by the very mothers and fathers who have seen their children die – and keep quiet about it. If I hear it, the world will know it as long as I can speak. And I want you to remember that that is your responsibility as well.

The responsibility to defend those who are defenceless, to speak for those who are voiceless, to make sure that the world understands what is happening, and to make sure that we in this country are aware of what is happening, is not the responsibility of only one or two people. It is our joint responsibility.

Because I have done this, the Minister has called me a liar and a slanderer. He must take responsibility for those words. I have in my possession affidavits, and I will read simply a few examples of what has happened to people during the last few months since the police and the military invaded the townships and since we have had this unrest.

There was a little boy called Walter Pule Makhata, a schoolboy aged fourteen from Naledi, Soweto. He went to the shop to buy a loaf of bread, was hit by birdshot and found dead.

In Katlehong, three children, one of them mentally

retarded, were allegedly assaulted by police on 13th September 1984. The police fired tear gas into the house and walked in, asking where the children were. When they found them, they started to kick and hit them all over their bodies. This happened to children.

On 15th August an unnamed boy (he refused to give his name, but called himself A.B.), aged fifteen, was on the roof of his house in Watville, Benoni, with two other people, making repairs. There were no apparent disturbances in the area at that time. Then the police came through shooting tear-gas cylinders. Some people ran from the street into A.B.'s house for shelter. The other two men on the roof fled but he lay down on the roof. A policeman mounted the ladder to the roof, came up to him and discharged a tear-gas cylinder into his face. He has lost his left eye as a result. If this is not an atrocity, what is? And if the Minister does not know it, he must make it his business to know it.

Nicholas Mldulwa, ten years old, was sent out by his father one evening to fetch firewood. The area was so quiet that his father actually thought this was safe to do. A Combi came by, a shot was fired. The father ran out and found his boy hit on the left side of his forehead with a rubber bullet. The police came and told him to keep the matter quiet. He refused, went to the lawyers, and he signed an affidavit. He even gave the registration number of the vehicle.

Elsie Nana, nineteen years old, was arrested on 3rd October while attending a prayer vigil. She was told to write a statement and give details about whatever she knew about the activities of other people. When she told them she was two months pregnant, she was assaulted – repeatedly kicked and hit with a sjambok [a rubber baton] on her stomach.

All of this the Minister can ask of the people who

have made these affidavits. All I want to ask him is, *"Who is the Liar?* Who is the slanderer? Who is the one who is trying to cover up deeds like these?" As long as these things happen and as long as we hear about it, it will be our responsibility to testify against the evil that is gripping this country.

We will not be silent. We will not stop doing this. We will refuse to be intimidated. It seems to me that the South African government thinks that these atrocities will stop us from demanding our freedom. But the South African government must learn that the time when they can avert change, fundamental change, in South Africa by merely reaching for a gun is over. We will no longer be silenced by fear, or by intimidation, or even by the wanton killing of our people. The demands are there, and are clear: release the political prisoners; unban the organizations; scrap all these laws that have made South Africa a hell for so many people to live in; stop killing our children and our people on the streets; let us participate in an open democratic society – then there will be peace in this country, and they must know that.

And so the state threatens to ban the organizations, and it threatens to ban the United Democratic Front. It will be a little difficult, because the UDF, I have often said, *is* the people of South Africa, and they cannot ban the people. The UDF embodies the dreams of the people of South Africa, and they cannot ban that dream. The UDF embodies the aspirations of the people toward a free and just society, and they cannot ban that. They can do whatever they want, but the determination of our people to be free will remain and will become the real reality that even government will have to face. And so it seems to me that all of the threats will not really in the end help the South African government. . . .

The most important thing is what I want you to

remember tonight: what we are fighting for, what we are struggling for. What our people are suffering for, what our people are dying for – that is worthwhile. Let us not give that up. Let us remember that no threat and no form of intimidation and no trick that the system can play on any one of us, including myself, can bring us to the point where we will be silenced, where we will accept the situation as it is, because if we do that we might as well give up and die. We sometimes die a thousand times before we die, because when we are afraid we die every day a little bit. We die in our humanity, we die in our determination, and we die in our self-respect. Let us not come to that point.

For me, it is clear I have experienced in this last year something within the community of the UDF that will remain with me as long as I live. I have experienced support, and I have experienced a determination, and I have experienced a love for freedom that is a precious gift that we have. We must not give that up, and this is what we have to continue to work for. I have seen a new South Africa. I have seen a land not of apartheid; not of death; not of chains; but a land of joy and a land of freedom and a land of peace. Let us fight for that land.

And I have seen a new land where our children will no longer be bowed down by the yolk of racism. Let us fight for that land.

I have seen a land where our people will work and enjoy the fruits of their labour. Let us fight for that land.

I have seen a land where families will no longer be broken up and where mothers and fathers will enjoy the love and the respect of their children. Let us fight for that land.

I have seen a land where the misery of relocation is

no more, and where the graves dug for little children who will tomorrow die of hunger remain empty. Let us fight for that land.

I have seen a land where those of us who fight for freedom, and for justice and for the self-respect of this country, will no longer be sent to prison, will no longer be tortured, will no longer be threatened, will no longer be shot on the streets of our nation, but will be rewarded with honour and with the presence of justice. Let us fight for that land.

And I have seen a land where we, together, will build something that is worthwhile, that is faithful to what we believe. Let us not give that up, but make tonight a new dedication for that moment. Because I believe it does not matter what happens now. I believe that the freedom that we have struggled for, and the freedom that we have died for, will become a reality. *You* can make it happen.

9

If This Is Treason,
I Am Guilty

This speech was given at a gathering of the UDF in
Durban on 27th February 1985.

*

We have entered a decisive phase in our struggle.
Those of us who have warned that the South African
government cannot be trusted, that the reforms they
are talking about are cosmetic, that apartheid and
racism still reign supreme, and that the South African
government still has only one goal, namely absolute
power for itself and for the white minority and continued control over the majority of our people in this
country – those of us who have warned of that were
right. Subsequent events, since we have begun to
make this clear, have shown that this government
indeed cannot be trusted. While the South African
government talked of reforms and while they were
engaged in a massive effort to mislead the international community, they instituted a racist constitution. While they were talking about reform they
continued the homelands policy. While they were
talking about reform they continued the de-
nationalization of South Africa's people, robbing our
black people of their birthright and of their right to

stay in this land. While they were talking about reforms they continued their forced removals, their policies of subtle genocide by forcing our people from the lands where they had lived for so many years into those concentration camps the South African government calls relocation areas. While they were talking about reform and while they were signing peace treaties with countries like Mozambique, they detained us, they shot at our people, they tear gassed us when we peacefully, so powerfully demonstrated our rejection of their policies and of their constitution. While they were talking about peace with other nations they sent their police and their troops into our townships, they broke up our funeral services with violence, they threatened our unarmed people, and they murdered our children on the streets of the townships. While they were talking about reform and while they were lying to the world, saying that apartheid is dead, the unrest all over the country proved that the struggle for justice and our struggle for genuine liberation shall continue. The boycott not only proved the discontent of our people but it also proved the determination of our people. And these are the things that the South African government cannot even begin to understand or begin to stop. While they spouted their propaganda across the world we proved to the world and to the government that neither smear campaigns nor dogs nor guns nor tear gas can undermine the determination of our people to be free.

So now the South African government is in trouble. They don't know what to do. There is no direction, there is no sense of where they are going. If you go and ask the people who sit in parliament what it is that they want before the end of this year, no one will be able to tell you, because they don't know what they want. There is such a state of confusion that one is justified in saying that not since Sharpeville in 1960 was the South African government so vulnerable to pressure, so confused, as now. There is no control over the economy – and you know the reason the rand is so low is that it has become so expensive to live abroad these days.

So they are worried because they have this new constitution, and with all their pomp and splendour they have opened the new parliament. Now they have their three "parliaments": they have the whites on one side and the coloureds on another side, and they have the Indians on another side. And the thing is not working – and that is the problem of course. While they are there they are supposed to govern this country. They are supposed to take note of what is happening, and they are supposed to think about this and to make intelligent noises about it. They are supposed to see the problems of our country, and to try to find solutions because that is what they are there for – so they say. Indeed you know the problems facing South Africa. We have unrest in this land that has not stopped since it began in the middle of 1984. There is a rising cost of living that cannot be stopped by the government either: the general sales tax will go up, essential subsidies will be dropped, the salaries of the new MP's will have to be paid, their new homes will have to be paid for. There is a tax relief for the rich. They were supposed to pay extra tax on all those perks that they have – all those expensive cars, and homes, and things – and the government said, "Oh no. Oh no, this is very difficult, and we can't do that. We will have to wait a few years to implement this policy." Who do you think is going to pay the eight hundred million rand that the South African government is losing because the rich are not going to be taxed? *You* are going to pay it, the people will have to pay it. This is not something that is being discussed. Crossroads is burning – eighteen people are dead. The war in Namibia continues – three million rand a day is spent on the government's illegal occupation of that country they should have been out of long ago. They are not discussing that.

Here in our own land there is a crisis in education. Our children are not going to school – and there are very good reasons for that – but they are not talking about that. What are they talking about? You saw in the newspapers: the thing they are discussing is the case of those white MP's who may or may not have had a Hottentot for a grandfather sometime. That is what they are talking about. And in the middle of this bankruptcy, the state president makes an announcement – although not for our consumption, because we know the government and we don't believe them even when they say these things; this is for the United States and for Britain. The state president says, "From now on the government will actually recognize that there will be a permanent presence of black people in the urban areas." We can now actually live in South Africa. That is what they say. "And therefore there will be a cabinet committee who will look into the possibilities of these black people being able to participate in the affairs of the government within the framework of the new constitution."

If the state president makes the announcement that black people can actually live in South Africa now, and the government will recognize them, what does he expect us to think? They actually expect us to sit back and be very happy and be very grateful and to say, "Ja, dankie baas . . ." [Yes, thank, you boss]. Doesn't he

know that black people have been here long before he
came here, that black people belong in this country,
and that we will be here long after he goes back, and
doesn't he know that this land is not his to give us –
that this land is ours and will one day again belong to
us?

We are not grateful for these little concessions that
they make. We are merely saying to the state president
and to his government, Do not fool yourselves now.
Don't go around trying to fool the world, because
certainly you cannot fool us – we know where we
belong!

The problem that we have to face is how we can in
this situation keep the initiative that we have gained.
The fact is that international pressure is growing; in
the United States, in spite of constructive engagement
– maybe also because of constructive engagement –
there is an unprecedented movement of protest
against the South African government and its policies,
and against constructive engagement. Never before
have people in the USA been so engaged in solidarity
with the people of South Africa. And this will happen
again and again and again. They are engaged in the
struggle not simply because they feel like it, but because you, the people of South Africa, are engaged in
the struggle, and you have made them see that it is
worthwhile for them to throw their weight behind us.
And that is important.

All over Europe the movement against apartheid is
growing. I spoke not so long ago to a new organization
called Western European Parliamentarians for Action
against Apartheid, and they have pledged themselves
to try to put pressure on their own governments, and
through them to put as much pressure as possible on
the South African government so that fundamental

change can take place. These people are doing that because in South Africa there are people who believe in the struggle, who fight for what we believe in, who believe in justice, who believe in liberation, and who believe that we ought to be participating in that struggle. As long as you are involved, the people of the world will more and more become involved. To the chagrin of the South African government, President Kaunda goes around the world and asks for pressure on the South African government and calls for disinvestment. The Danish government this morning announced that it will no longer allow its companies to bring new investment to South Africa. The campaign is working.

In response to this unprecedented international pressure the South African government is trying to show that it is really changing, so they say that Nelson Mandela can come out of jail and that Walter Sisulu can come out of jail. But while they say to Walter Sisulu, "Please come out of jail", and to Nelson Mandela, "Please come out of jail", they take Sisulu's wife and put *her* in prison. And they take fifteen other people and put *them* in prison. What is the matter with this government? You know, our problem in this country is really that we sit with a government that can only think so far. There must really be people in that government who cannot think very well. One wonders where they went to school; if we knew, we could go talk to those schools and say, "If you turn out any further governments for this country, please advise us."

I noticed something when the government made Nelson Mandela the offer of release. A magazine in this country wrote that Mandela should accept that offer because in doing so he would not endear himself to the people who now want to claim him – like the United Democratic Front. He would instead establish his credibility with all the peace-loving, thinking people in South Africa, namely "them". I read that article and I thought, What a cheek! Who are they now to claim Mandela for themselves? They are the ones who created policies which made it impossible for black people to live in this country like decent human beings. They are the ones who, when we started to resist these policies, made laws that made it impossible for us even to take the first step of saying, "This is our situation; this is our land; we want to live here as people recognized as citizens". Then they banned his organization, they drove him to violence, they locked him up for twenty-two years, they banned and banished his wife, they locked up in Robben Island and the prisons of this country the people who worked with him, they called him a terrorist, they called him a communist – and now, when they are in difficulty, they want to offer him a conditional release and say that we must not claim him because he must establish his credibility with them. Mandela does not need to establish his credibility with those people. Mandela does not need to establish his credibility with anyone but the people who are still in the struggle for justice and liberation in this country, and with them he is already established.

But of course, since the South African government is facing all this difficulty, someone has to get the blame. This time it is the turn of the United Democratic Front. The Minister of Law and Order made a speech last night. As usual, it was a speech that was full of threats, and intimidation, and promises of more intimidation. And he singled out, again, the United Democratic Front as an organization that is creating a climate of revolution in South Africa. I want to say to the Minister: "The people of South Africa are getting a little tired of these threats. We are engaged in a struggle for liberation, not because we want to die, but because we want our people to be free. We are engaged in a struggle for liberation, not because we wish to die, but because you oppress us, and as long as you continue to oppress us we will have to resist. We are people, and we are people who belong in this land. The climate of revolution Mr Minister, is not created by those who struggle for justice and peace, but the climate of revolution in this country is created by those who make policies that despise and undermine the human dignity of people. The climate of revolution is created by those who make policies that exploit our people, that take away the necessities of the many to give luxuries to the few. The climate of revolution is created by those who make policies that create hunger and starvation in the homelands while the tables of the rich in white South Africa are sagging with food that will be thrown in the dustbin. The climate of revolution is not created by the United Democratic Front, but by those people like you, Mr Minister, who refuse to listen to the voice of reason, who refuse to listen to our people when they say we want our rights, and we want them here, and we want them now, because they are our rights. The climate of revolution is not created by the United Democratic Front, but by those people like you who detain without trial; by those who allow our people to be tortured in their jails; by those who allow the wanton killing of our people on the streets of our nation." These are the things that are creating a climate of revolution in our nation, and the Minister must not blame the United Democratic Front — he must put the blame where it belongs, right in front of the door of the South African government, of which he is a part.

Now the government has charged some of our brothers and sisters with treason. As I have said over and over again, this is a serious charge. Treason is described as organizing, or taking part in, or instigating, armed revolt in order to overthrow the government. Actually, they are being charged under a section of the Internal Security Act in which any act of subversion – which can include speaking out against the South African government or calling for pressure on it – is also treason. It is wide, it is irresponsible, but it is a law that is on the statute books of this country. So these people will be charged with treason.

I consider this a scandalous, dastardly, and cowardly act. I have worked for a long time with the people who are being charged. I have not heard them call for violence. From its inception, the United Democratic Front has been an organization committed to nonviolence. Under the most difficult circumstances, we did not ask people to take up arms. We said to our people, Let us find ways and means, with all of the odds against us, even at this late hour, to try peacefully to express our legitimate political aspirations in this country.

We know that we have had a long battle behind us. We know that every single effort toward peaceful change in this country has been met by the government with violence and ended by a massacre. We know how our people marched peacefully on 21st March now twenty-five years ago in Sharpeville. One day soon we shall be commemorating that tragic event, when their peaceful demonstration ended in bloodshed, most of them shot in the back. We know that in 1976 our children took to the streets with nothing in their hands except placards which said to the South African police: "We do not want to fight. Please release our comrades and friends." Those children were shot down by the police by the hundreds. And we know that in 1980 in Cape Town our children took up the challenge and marched peacefully for a better future for themselves, expressing only that they do not want to grow up in a country where racism is rife, and where oppression is the order of the day, and where exploitation is around every corner, and where our people are being pushed into little holes in the homelands where they will die of hunger and despair. The answer the South African government gave once again was guns, and dogs and tear gas – and our children died, and you will remember the policeman's words when little Bernard Fortuin, ten years old, was shot on the streets of Elsies River (see p. 78) – the words that reverberated around the world, to the shame of South Africa: "Let the bastard die!"

And now, in 1984, we have formed the United Democratic Front and have said to people, "Let us not despair; let us not say that the only answer to the South African government's violence is violence; let us not seek to repay them with the same things that they are doing to us; let us not seek to be overcome with evil, but indeed to find a way to overcome evil with good by peacefully demonstrating what it is that we want." We made this organization into a force that even the whole world will now have to reckon with. We never picked up a single stone, but they came again with their dogs and their guns and their bazookas, and they killed our people even on the night of the election. We in the United Democratic Front said, "Let us try to find ways of telling our young people to commit themselves once again, even now, to a strategy of nonviolence." And we did, and the world respects the United Democratic Front for it. It was the South African government who turned around and detained our people. It was the South African government who turned around and sent their police to our demonstrations on the night of the election, and it was they who started again to shoot at our people. What is it that we have done? We in the United Democratic Front have created a unity that this country has not seen for almost three decades. We brought back the spirit of the struggle that we knew in the 1950s. We were the people who were able to bring people together even in this racist land – where hatred is the order of the day because hatred is the theme of the South African government – to make it possible for black and white to work together in the face of strong criticism from others. We have been able to say to people: "Do not look at the matter simply by the colour of a person's skin, but try to judge in terms of that person's commitment to the struggle for justice and liberation." And we have succeeded in doing that.

In one single year, in a short twelve-month period, we have brought together a mass movement now representing millions of people in this land. We have challenged the South African government's constitution, and what is more, we have won. We have made people aware of their rights in South Africa. We thereby exposed the violent, oppressive nature of this government. We have given the people of this land back their self-respect, we have given them a faith in the justice of our struggle, we have given them a belief that we shall overcome. This is the United Democratic Front. We stand for things that the South African government cannot understand. We stand for democracy. They don't know the meaning of the word. We stand for nonracialism. They cannot stand it when people of different races can live and work together. We stand for an open democratic society. They cannot stand it, because then they know that their violence will have come to an end.

But there is something more. We must ask the question, Is what we have done treason? I have called for the foundation and the formation of the United Democratic Front. I have spoken more than anybody else over the last year. I have said publicly that apartheid is evil, that it is a blasphemy, that it is a heresy. I have said that the South African government is unjust. I have said that this government is undemocratic, it is unrepresentative, it does not have the love or the support of the people, it has no right to exist, it is illegitimate, it should not be there. I have said openly that the South African government is a violent government. I have called for Christians and people of other faiths to pray for the downfall of the South African government, to pray that God should give us another government, to pray that God should remove them. I have from the very beginning resisted this government on the basis of my Christian commitment and of my Christian faith. And I shall continue to do so as long as God gives me breath in my body. If this is treason, then I am guilty of treason, and I would say to the South African government tonight, if I am guilty of treason, then charge me with treason and put me in jail.

I say this not out of a sense of bravado. I say this not out of defiance, because I know that the Minister to whom I am speaking now is a very powerful man, a man without a conscience who can do whatever he likes and get away with it. But I say this because in a perverted, unjust and cruel society such as ours, where those who fight for freedom and peace and human dignity are banned, detained, and charged with treason while criminals sit in Parliament and receive accolades from those who share in their power and privilege, this is the only decent thing to do. And if I have committed treason by resisting the South African government – which is exactly what our brothers and sisters who are now in jail have done – then the South African government must now put me in jail and charge me with treason too.

But you must know that we are indeed in the beginning of a decisive phase of our struggle in the history of our land. This is the beginning of the end of apartheid. Its days are numbered. And what you must do, Mr Minister, you must do quickly, for your day of judgement is near. You must remember that the struggle does not depend on one or two or three or four people, and that the strength of the United Democratic Front has always been that we do not simply depend on those people that we have put in positions of leadership. The strength of the United Democratic Front has always been the people, has always been their commitment, has always been their participation in the struggle. So in the end it is not a question of whether the UDF will survive the onslaught because a few of the leaders are in jail facing trial, but in the end it is a question of whether you, its members, in your own commitment will remain faithful. Do not begin to fear the future, do not begin to give up faith in our struggle and in the justice of our cause. Do not be overcome by the evil that this government represents, but overcome evil with good.

So in the midst of trial and tribulation I exhort you to remain a faithful people. In the midst of the hopelessness and despair that sometimes overcomes us because we think that the powers standing over against us are so invincible – remain a hopeful people. In the midst of fear and uncertainties that come up in our own hearts because we do not know what tomorrow will bring, and we do not exactly know what will happen to us inside those jails or whether we will even come out alive – be a strong people. In the midst of unfaithfulness by so many who turn around and for a mess of pottage sell the birthright of our people just to sit in a bogus parliament and be given power and honour by people who do not even know the meaning of the words – be a committed people. And in the midst of the violence of this South African government which will continue and which will increase because they have created the monster that in the end is destined to devour even themselves, in the midst of the destruction that may come – remain a peace-loving people. In the midst of the madness of racism and hatred that still reign in this country – be a compassionate people. And in the end, if we remain faithful, if we take the risks that are necessary, and if we remain committed to what we believe in, we will be also a victorious people!

10

In the Name of Jesus

On 16th June 1985, the ninth anniversary of the Soweto uprising, the South African Council of Churches held in Cape Town a Service of Prayer for the End to Unjust Rule. Allan Boesak preached this sermon on that occasion.

*

> If we are being called to account today for an act of kindness shown to a cripple and are asked how he was healed, then know this, you and everyone else in Israel, it is by the name of Jesus Christ of Nazareth whom you crucified but whom God raised from the dead that this man stands before you completely healed. Salvation is found in no one else, for there is no other name under heaven given to us, by which we must be saved.
>
> Acts 4:9, 10 and 12

Brothers and sisters, people of God, we are still in the season of Pentecost, and this reminds us of the out-pouring of God's power in the Holy Spirit, the empowerment of God's people so that we are lifted up, raised up as it were, strengthened to fear no longer, to look no longer over our shoulder with anxiety, to ask no longer what will happen to us if we dare speak or if we are known as followers of Jesus. We are raised up to enjoy the freedom and the fearlessness of the children of God, for all those who know the empowerment of the Spirit will no longer bow under the threat of intimidation or under fear. Those who know the power of the Spirit of God will no longer watch anxiously or ask anxiously, "What will happen to me?" but will only ask, "What is it, Lord, that you want me to do?"

So with Pentecost the people are challenged and changed. We read of thousands of conversions. But something more happens; society and the world are disturbed and transformed, everybody knows that something extraordinary is happening. You can see how wonderful it is that God is working in the world, for then, and this is inevitable, comes the confrontation with the powers that be.

If people are being changed, if the structures of the world are being confronted, if the very world itself is faced with the challenge to be transformed, then no longer hatred but love shall rule, no longer fear but boldness shall rule, no longer injustice but justice shall rule. Powers which are built upon injustice must be ended, but these powers get upset and disturbed, they get angry, and so they call the apostles to account. They want to know what is happening here: "By what name, by what power are you doing this?" Chapters 3, 4 and 5 of Acts tell us how this drama unfolds.

At first the Church is very hesitant. Quietly Peter and John put the case. They do not want to be too direct; they say, "You must judge for yourselves, you must make your own decisions whether it is right in God's sight to obey yourself rather than God." As the situation develops, as the confrontation grows, and as the challenge can no longer be avoided both on the side of the powers and on the side of the apostles, a new answer comes. We hear the Church pray, "Now, Lord, consider the oppressed and enable Your servants to speak Your word with great boldness." Later it is even more clear, much more poignant and indeed unequivocal: "We must obey God more than man", and so what you do to us is *your* decision; if you want to throw us in jail it is *your* decision; if you want to give us into the hands of the Romans in order to be killed as you killed Jesus it is *your* decision. However, as far as we are concerned "we must obey God more than man".

This is the key verse. It is this verse which rings like a bell in the history of the Christian Church whenever it is faced with persecution. It is a verse that has people lifted up, ordinary, weak, human beings, and makes them stand firm and say with Martin Luther, "Here I stand. I can do no other". It is the verse that comes after all that John Calvin said in his books, in all the long chapters he wrote about the Christian attitude towards the state and the government and those in authority. After he has said, "Yes, we must obey them", "Yes, they are not bad by nature", "Yes, they might be good", "Yes, we must listen to them", "Yes, we must trust them", "Yes, we must help them". After all this he says, "But you must remember before all else – we are called to obey God more than man".

However, this verse must and can only be understood in the light of the portion that we have read: "There is no other name given under heaven by which there is salvation, and you must know that what we do we do in the name of Jesus Christ of Nazareth whom you have killed and God has raised up from the dead." This is the basis of Christian faith and Christian obedience. It is the foundation of the risk that Christians must take in the world, the foundation of all action by Christians in the world. By what power, by what name, do you do this? There is only one answer:

"In the name of Jesus of Nazareth." Note here that Peter, as he does so often in chapters 2, 3, 4 and 5 of Acts, says to these people, "the one you have crucified". This is not an anti-Semitic challenge justifying discrimination against the Jewish community for having killed Jesus. "No," Peter says, "you must understand that you thought that he was dead but God has raised him up and he is alive *now*, and his name is alive. You thought that you had disposed of him, but he is alive and his name is a source of power and inspiration for his people who believe in him."

This name, this name of Jesus, what name is this? It is the same name Moses heard that day when he stood in the desert and watched the flame devouring the bush, yet the flame would not go out. It is the name of the God of the Exodus, it is the name of the God who told us, "I am what I am; I am there for My people; I have heard their cry and I have seen their suffering, how they are bent low under the whip, under the yoke of slavery in Egypt. Therefore I shall come down and deliver them from the hands of the king of Egypt." In this name Moses challenged Pharaoh and told him in no uncertain terms, "Let my people go". It is the same name Moses invoked when the people of Israel saw the sea parting so they could walk through it. It is the same name under which Israel marched through the wilderness, the fire by night and the cloud by day to guide them. When they were hungry it was *that* name which gave them food, and when they were thirsty it was *that* name which gave them water. It was in the name of God that the prophets took up, so clearly, the cause of the poor, the weak, the oppressed and the needy. In this name Elijah challenged King Ahab, "Thus says the Lord, you have killed and also taken possession; in the place where dogs lick up the blood of

Naboth shall dogs lick your own blood." This was the word of the Lord to a king who did not understand justice and mercy and compassion, who robbed his people of their land and then turned around and killed them. In this name Jeremiah said to King Joachim, "Do justice and righteousness, deliver from the hand of the oppressor those who have been wronged. But you, you King Joachim, you have eyes and heart only for dishonest gain, for shedding innocent blood, and for practising oppression and violence. You shall die and your people shall not cry for you." In this name Ezekiel spoke of judgement to the rulers of Israel:

> Shepherds of Israel, you do not feed my sheep, the weak you have not strengthened, the sick you have not healed, the crippled you have not bound up, the strayed you have not brought back, the lost you have not sought. With falseness and harshness you have ruled over them. Thus says the Lord: Behold, I am against those shepherds, and I will rescue My sheep from their bonds. You shall no longer eat My sheep. I will seek the lost, I will bring back the strayed, I will bind up the crippled, I will strengthen the weak, and I will feed them with justice.

This is the name in which prophets have to stand up and speak to the people, but this is also the name in which prophets have to stand up and speak the Word of God to rulers who do not want to listen, who consistently disobey God's laws, who persist in oppression and in violence. This is the name that has become alive in Jesus of Nazareth. This is the name which proclaims sight for the blind, liberty for the captives, and good news for the poor. This name is power and love, justice and mercy.

When we called for a day of prayer to remove unjust structures of oppression in this country and for the removal of those who continue to do injustice to God's people, who continue to live off the suffering and oppression of God's people in this country, there were many people who were upset. There were people who talked about churches that have been divided by this call. The press has used this for its own political ends, and to this day South African television has refused to broadcast the second of the statements of the South African Council of Churches, in which the Council very clearly said that it affirms the call for this day. I have seen articles in newspapers that I never would have dreamed would be published, secular newspapers that spoke the propaganda of the South African government day by day, that often do not even know how to spell the name Jesus. They have offered to pray for us because we are so misguided.

Yet this has been one of the most affirmative signs that we are right; because they are so desperate, it must be close to the bone. Today we say to them, "We will not take up our guns against you. We will not ask people, as you do, to go out on the streets of the nation and shoot people down like dogs. We will not ask God to bless our guns as you did on 16th December so that you could kill other people and then rob the land." When we made this call we were very clear. I said that day in Johannesburg that we do not believe in the power of violence, but that we believe in the power of prayer. They know this and that is why they are upset, that is why they are angry, that is why they are fearful. They know that the God we worship is a living God, He is a powerful God, He is a God of justice. This God will not turn away from His people, this God will rise up, this God will deliver us from the hands of those evil men who think and do violence to God's defenceless people. I believe that this will *happen*. So when they ask us, By which power do you do this? By which name do you do this? we will say, "We do this in the name of this Jesus who taught us what God is like".

The people who have challenged us, the people who have said we are asking for violence, the people who are angry with us; those are the people who do not *know* what it means to suffer because of the colour of your skin. They do not *know* what it means to be in jail because you do not have a pass book. They do not *know* what it means to sit under sheets of plastic in Crossroads when the rains of the Cape winter fall. They do not *know* what it means to bury your children who die of hunger in this land where there is so much wealth. They do not *know* what it means to get up in the morning and not know whether by night you will be in jail or back with your family. They do not *know* what it means to live in so-called white South Africa for eleven months of the year and return for three weeks at the end of the year to your homeland, to your family where you are a stranger to your own children. Because they do not know this, because they do not feel this pain, because it is impossible for them to feel our pain, they say to us, "By what name and by what power do you do this, who gave you the right?" We will say as humbly but as clearly as we can, "By the name of Jesus whom you have killed, but whom God has raised up – in his name are we doing this."

Peter's testimony was a theological issue, but at the same time it was a political issue, for he was dragged before the senate, the highest civil authority for the Jewish population at that time. They were the people who had been entrusted with some political power by the Romans. We know this from letters the Romans sent to Jerusalem which always began in this way: "To the government, the senate, and the people of Jerusalem." They were under the system the Romans had devised; they were responsible for law and order and for religion – for all Jewish issues. One could almost say they were responsible for their "own affairs" in Jerusalem. Jesus of Nazareth was executed by the Romans because they regarded him to be a rebel against Caesar. Caesar proclaimed himself lord; he called himself the saviour of the people. Jesus of Nazareth came and said, "No, that is not the truth. I *am* the Saviour of the people, I *am* Lord, God has made *me* so for the Spirit of the Lord is upon me." Caesar could not understand that; Caesar could not tolerate that, so Jesus in his love and in his mercy and his justice became a threat to the political power of Caesar, and by the same token became a threat to the political power of the prophets of Caesar in Jerusalem. You see, our struggle did not begin yesterday or in 1960 or in 1910; it is an old, old story.

Now this Jesus, who had been killed because he dared call himself Lord, his name is alive again, and Peter stands up and proclaims, "Therefore let all Israel be assured of this: God has made this Jesus whom you crucified Lord and Christ." This is a political statement, and it becomes, therefore, a political threat. They thought they had disposed of him, but no, here they are confronted by him once again, through the life and the witness of a small, weak, but very clear little Church. Yes, the name of Jesus Christ brings healing, the name of Jesus Christ brings power, the name of Jesus Christ brings transformation in the world; but it also brings confrontation with the powers of evil in this world. It is a powerful name, but it is also a vulnerable name; it can be misused and betrayed.

In the name of Jesus, the Christian Church so often

in our history has forsaken the poor, the weak and the needy. It has become a Church where the poor no longer feel comfort nor any challenge to their own situation. Is it not the fault of our own lives that the Church or religion has become the opium of the people; the fault of the Church that it is afraid to walk in the footsteps of her Lord who said, "Those who take up the sword shall perish by the sword"? In the name of Jesus the Church justified racism and apartheid in this country. Using biblical verses it built a theology around apartheid, defending it on biblical grounds in the name of Jesus. In our country people are despised, in the name of Jesus, because of the colour of their skin.

This government says it is a Christian government. We have a new constitution which begins with the proclamation of Christian faith, a constitution which says that it is to uphold Christian standards; yet this Christian constitution deprives us of our human dignity and our human rights. In South Africa families are broken up for the sake of economic gain and exploitation, and starvation wages are being paid. In the eastern Cape I have heard that even today, on farms in the areas around Humansdorp and Jansenville, our people earn six rand a month, ten rand a month, fifteen rand a month. The age of slavery is *not* over. And in this country the people's birthright is being taken away. . . . In this country the greed of the few guarantees an ongoing poverty for the masses of our people. In this country it is not love and justice but hatred and fear that rules supreme. In this country our people say, "We can no longer stand this; we can no longer take this suffering; we can no longer watch our children die. We will rise up, and we will say that apartheid is wrong." When this happens they are banned like Johnnie Yssel or thrown in jail and tortured to death like Steve Biko and so many others. The strength of our nation are killed, mown down like dogs, as happened on bloody Thursday in Langa and Uitenhage. In the *name* of Jesus this is happening.

In the *name* of Jesus this is happening – in the *name* of Jesus. For as long as the people who rule this country and those who vote for them say that they are Christians, that they base themselves upon the word of God, that their word is a testimony to this Jesus whom we believe in and who died on the cross, the Christian Church must rise up and say, "No, it is not true. It is a *lie*. You betray the name of Jesus."

As long as this happens the Church must rise up and say, "You can claim what you want but we shall tell you what God says 'you shall not take my name in vain'." As long as this happens the Church must rise up and say, "You shall reap what you sow." As long as this happens the Church must rise up and say, "It is not those who say 'Lord, Lord', who will enter into the kingdom of heaven, but those who learn to do the will of my Father who is in heaven." No matter how many times you say, "I am a Christian", no matter how many times you read your Bible, no matter how many times you rise up in Parliament and say that we stand under almighty God, God's judgement will come down on you. The Church will say it, and I will say it today, not because I am better, not because I think I am stronger, not because we have power, but because it is God's own truth. And if the Church is afraid to speak God's truth then we might as well throw this Bible into the sea. So in the name of Jesus, the name of Jesus is being betrayed.

But the name of Jesus can never be used to justify exploitation, it can never be used to justify the wanton killing of our people, it can never be used to justify oppression and suffering. It is a name of power, it is a name of liberation, it is a name of love, it is a name of compassion, it is a name of justice, it is a name of peace. Those who know the name of Jesus know peace; those who know the name of Jesus know justice, and they will stand up and fight. In this name we stand, in this name we pray for justice and for peace, in this name we pray for the crumbling of unjust structures. I think that they are shouting so loudly out there because they do not want us to hear already the crumbling of the walls. In this name we shall have faith; in this name we shall continue to pray and continue to make ourselves available to God.

To pray does not mean that I will now fold my hands and close my eyes and sit back and let God do all the work. To pray means that I will say to God, "I am now at your disposal. *Use* me: use me for *peace*, use me for *justice*, use me for *compassion*, use me for *mercy*, use me for *love*, use me for *liberation* so that your people can see." I believe that God will hear us as we pray for the removal of those who persist in disobeying God's will. I believe that God has *seen* us. I believe that God will *hear* us. I believe that God will *use* us.

And so, my brothers and sisters gathered for this prayer service today, let us look upon the name of Jesus which spells peace and love, mercy and justice, compassion and freedom. Let us stand in the name of Jesus. Let us believe that this land will one day be a land where we can live in peace with one another. Let us believe that this land will become a land where we will no longer be looked down upon because of the colour of our skin. Let us believe that this land will become a land where there is security for our children, and that it will lie in our love and our search for justice and not in guns and tanks and police forces. This land will become a land in which we shall be able to build up God's kingdom and all that is part of that kingdom. Because we believe this, we shall stand, we shall be clear, we shall be counted, we shall speak so that they can hear from Cape Town to Pretoria, from Port Elizabeth to Durban, from any little hovel in this country to the highest councils of authority. "Our Father," we will say, "who art in heaven, give us, all our people, our daily bread so that we will not die of hunger. And forgive us our sins, even that sin of being afraid to stand up and be counted for justice, and we will forgive those that trespass against us. And lead us not into temptation, but deliver us from evil. For *Thine* is the kingdom, for *Thine* is the power, for *Thine* is the glory for ever and ever. Amen."

11

If South Africa Had Listened

On 26th June 1955 a coalition of South Africans opposed to apartheid signed a document called the Freedom Charter. This speech was given on the thirtieth anniversary of that event.

*

I want today to try to understand what it means that we in this country have a document called the Freedom Charter. It is a document that we can be rightly proud of. Indeed, it is a document that represents, better than any other document ever written in this country, the political aspirations of our people. It represents the dream of South Africa's people. It represents what it is that we want. It represents what we long for. It represents the expression of our desires about what kind of country we want. No other document, whether it was thought up by the British government, or whether it was drafted by the Nationalist government, or whether it was drafted by any other political party in this country, has ever been able so to capture the imagination of our people and so to inspire us in the struggle for justice, for freedom, and for liberation.

Today, 26th June 1985, it has been exactly thirty years since the people of this country, black and white together, came to Kliptown to formulate what has become known as the Freedom Charter. The Freedom Charter is the most democratic document that we know.

In this document we hope, and I hope, that our young people of today will find the necessary inspiration to continue to work and fight for a South Africa which one day will reflect the desires that live in the hearts of our people.

Let me remind you of the preamble to the Freedom Charter. It is so beautiful. Listen to these words:

> We the people of South Africa declare for all our country and all the world to know:
>
> – That South Africa belongs to all who live in it, black and white, and that no government can justly claim authority, unless it is based on the will of the people.
> – That our people have been robbed of their birthright to land, liberty and peace by a form of government founded on injustice and inequality.
> – That our country will never be prosperous or free until all our people live in brotherhood, enjoying equal rights and opportunities.
> – That only a democratic state, based on the will of the people, can secure to all our people, the birthright without distinction of colour, race, sex or belief.
>
> and therefore, we the people of South Africa, black and white together, equals, countrymen and brothers, adopt this Freedom Charter, and we pledge ourselves to strive together sparing nothing of our strength and our courage, until the democratic changes here set out, have been won.

These are the words that have become a foundation upon which we have built our struggle. These are the words that have grown to cosmic proportions; these are the words that eclipse even now the roar of the guns and the troop-carriers in our townships. Even above the clatter of the violence of the South African government, even above the cries of violence and fear that emanate from those people who want to maintain oppression in South Africa, we hear the sound of the Freedom Charter. Even above the laws that they make, that they try to force down our throats, we hear the words of the Freedom Charter. And even above the speeches that are being made by the state president and all those people he has put in power, even to those stooges in the coloured parliament, we hear the words of the Freedom Charter. And while these words, my brothers and sisters, inspire us, and while these words make us rise to every occasion, and while these words spell out for us the path that we have dedicated ourselves to walk without fear, and with clarity of mind, while we have this, we understand. So let the people of Britain and the United States see how the young people of South Africa come together to talk about this important document.

Let us think about what that means. It was young people who came together at the time that the Freedom Charter was adopted, at the time that our people, your fathers and mothers, those who have gone before us in the struggle, those who have said, even then, that we shall not give up until the day arrives that we and our children shall be free. When they came together the dismal record of this country, of oppression and dispossession and disenfranchisement, was already very, very clear. It was three hundred years old by then. They were living then under the constitution of 1910, a constitution which left no room for black people in this country to participate in the government, no room for black people in this country to help to shape the future of the land of their birth, no room for us to make our own contribution to make this country great. It was a constitution that excluded the majority of the people. They lived under a constitution that left room for further disenfranchisement, a constitution that left room for unjust structures and for Bantustan policies.

By then also apartheid was eight years old. By then they could already feel the damage that this system was doing to this country and to our people, and they could already begin to anticipate the damage that would be done to our people by it later. Already then, even when apartheid was only eight years old, they could see the irreparable damage done to race relations. Even then it was clear that the draconian laws that had been put on the statute books, laws like the Suppression of Communism Act, would not disappear, but would multiply. Even then they could see how this country would be shaped, not by hope, not by justice, and not by truth, but by lies and by despair and by the desperation of evil men who only knew the language of violence and threat and intimidation and racism. Even then, even when apartheid was only eight years old, others were already shaping what was to become known as the theology of apartheid. Even then, others were looking for arguments in the Bible that they could use to justify their oppression, so that they could continue to say "God is on our side". Even then, others were beginning to shape the lie that would become the core of the propaganda of the South African government.

Then, even as now, as our people came together to say "No" to this growing menace to our humanity, to say "No" to this monster that was being created by the people of this country who had the vote and who kept that government in power; even then as our people came together to seek a new future, to seek a new direction, to ask different questions, and to say, "We do not want this for ourselves; we do not want this for our children; we want a different land; we want another kind of future" – even then the meetings were broken up by police, as our meetings are today. Even then, our people were intimidated, as we are being intimidated today. I hear that first we had this hall we are meeting in tonight, then we were told we could not have the hall, then we were told again, yes, we can have the hall, and then we were told, no, we couldn't. And then the security police came here and tried to intimidate the people who said we could use the hall, so they would withdraw their permission. Ha! What do they think of our people? Do they think that we will really run away and say, "Oh yes, Baas. . . ." Don't they know that those days are over? Don't they know those days are long gone?

Even back then, they did what they do today. Even then, our people's homes were raided, as our homes are raided today. Even then, our people were detained, kept without trial, never charged. Even then, our people were tortured in their jails, as our people are tortured and murdered now. Even then, our leaders were banned and could not speak to us, as our people today face treason charges and are kept in jail and not allowed to stand up and speak the truth that comes from the heart of South Africa's oppressed and suffering people. Even then, the government was as afraid of that truth as they are now. Even then, they were as fearful of us as they are now – not because we hate them, not because we are going to kill them, but because they know injustice never pays. The day will come when they shall hear our words come true, because they know it is true: "You shall reap what you sow." That's why they are afraid.

So the charter came not out of the minds of people who sat behind desks and simply thought academically about the issue. The charter does not come out of a classroom situation. The Freedom Charter was not born in a discussion among academics. The Freedom Charter was born in the hearts of the people of this country who are oppressed. The Freedom Charter came out of our lives. The Freedom Charter is the child of our suffering, the child of our oppression; it is the child also of our hope and the child of our expectation of a better future for this country. The Freedom Charter could never have been born in a Nationalist government. The Freedom Charter could only have been born in the hearts of those who understand hypocrisy, who love freedom and who seek justice.

And so the moment the Freedom Charter was adopted the South African government said, "Communism! subversion! treason!" We learned then that it was subversive to say: "South Africa belongs to all its people." We learned then that it is treason to say: "Freedom in our lifetime." We learned then that it is treason to say: "Freedom for all." We learned then that it is treason to say to our people: "Let us rise up and let us act together so that we can establish freedom and humanity and decency in our land." The people who said that then were hauled before the courts of this land or thrown in jail or put on Robben Island, and some of them are still there – like Nelson Mandela.

But we have also learned some other things. We have learned that the same government who called our people communists and atheists because we believe in freedom, and the same people who therefore imply that we are not Christian, that we do not understand the Bible, that we do not know the name of Jesus – they are the people who betray his name. They betrayed the name of Jesus, for in the name of this Jesus – which is a name that spells liberation and freedom and humanity and justice and wholeness and reconciliation and peace – in this name, they have created apartheid. In this name they break up black family life. In this name, for economic gain and for the sake of exploitation, they create pass laws and influx control laws, and they separate men from their families, bring them into South Africa, and keep them here for eleven months of the year, so they can go back to their children and to their wives only at the end of the year for a measly three weeks, after they have become strangers to their own children. In the name of Jesus they did this. In the name of Jesus they stole our land, and they made us strangers in the land of our birth. In this name they pay starvation wages so that our people will remain poor. Our people are not poor because South Africa is poor. Our people are not poor because we do not want to work. Our people are poor because the rich are so rich, and our people are poor because we are consistently exploited and because we are consistently kept poor by a system that needs us to be poor.

In the name of Jesus these people have created Bantustans, those concentration camps the South African government euphemistically calls "relocation areas", where our old people die of despair and hopelessness and where our children die of hunger and malnutrition. They have done this. In the name of Jesus they sent their army into our townships; they sent their police into our townships; they shoot our people as if we were dogs. And in the name of Jesus they turn around and say that the police are not to blame. The South African government must know and they must understand. You cannot take the name of the Lord your God in vain. And one day they will pay for what they are doing to God's defenceless people in this country. They must understand that.

The same government that despises the Freedom Charter are the people who have systematically taken away whatever constitutional rights we have had. They are the people who then turned around and gave us dummy institutions like "Coloured Management Committees" and "Urban Bantu Councils" and an "Indian House of Delegates". Far from living up to their proclaimed democracy, they don't know the meaning of the word. The people who despise the Freedom Charter and who say the Freedom Charter is a document not suitable for South Africa are the ones who reject our participation and our contribution to this society. And they then create a new constitution, which is again built upon racism and which again entrenches apartheid and white minority rule, and they turn round and say to us: "You must go for this; you can participate; this is now a democracy." They must be joking.

And yet, we must ask, Why are they so afraid of the Freedom Charter? Why are they so afraid of the ideals of the Freedom Charter? They are people who look at the Freedom Charter and say: "This is not a good document: it is too vague, it is not radical enough, it is muddled thinking, it is not clear enough." But why then are they so afraid of it? Why can't we celebrate the Freedom Charter without interference? Why can't we talk about the Charter and why cannot the Charter become the basis for a new society in South Africa?

I will tell you why. They say that the things enshrined in the Freedom Charter are treason and subversion because it says that the people shall govern.

And the people shall govern – not some little group of white people who think that because they are white they have the right to govern everybody else. Not some little group of people who have been made honorary whites and can therefore sit in those "little houses" next to parliament and then say that they are parliament. But the people shall govern. Not the élite, not the rich, not the wealthy, not the clever, but the people shall govern – you will govern. That's why they are so afraid. It is not the army that shall govern, not the police that shall govern, not P. W. Botha who shall govern – *you* shall govern.

You see, what the Freedom Charter talks about is rights for everybody. The Freedom Charter says that all land shall be shared, it shall not belong to one little group, and it shall never again be divided on the 13 per cent or whatever else per cent basis. And there shall never be talk about white South Africa and Bantustans any more. The Freedom Charter says the doors of learning shall be open to all. No Bantu education any more, no *kleurling* education any more, no Indian education any more, no *Boere* education any more. The Freedom Charter says there shall be houses for all our people, there shall be decent shelter for all our people, but not while some people live in castles and in palaces while the masses of our people have to live in these shanties that they built in our townships, so they can come around and say, "Oh, aren't you lucky because look: you have a house!"

That is what the Charter says, and that is why they are so afraid. Because if these demands are met, then we will all be equal. And then if you go into a job you will be judged on your ability to work and not on the colour of your skin. Why are they afraid when we say that there shall be peace and there shall be friendship?

The question we must ask is: "Why is it a crime in South Africa to say there shall be peace and there shall be friendship?" It is because if you say there shall be peace, there can be no more apartheid. If you say there shall be peace, the army should not be in the townships. If you say there shall be peace, the police should not come out and kill our children. If you say there shall be peace, we shall all be equal before the law. If you say there shall be peace, we shall be paid for our work. If you say there shall be peace, those people who are in parliament now will not be in parliament. That is what it means. . . .

But all of this is treason; it is dangerous for the South African government because it is a government that is not a government of the people. It is a government based on injustice and oppression. It is a government that is not democratic, and the people in it are not representative; they are illegitimate, and therefore they ought not to be where they are.

That is why we came together on Sunday 16th June and we prayed to God: "Remove these people who are so unjust and who persist in disobeying Your will." And then they get angry and then they get upset – even the church leaders get upset. Why do they get upset? Do you know what they do? Every year on 16th December they get together and pray that God will bless their guns so that they can kill other people and steal their land. They pray for that. We do not pray for that. All we said was: "God, You see us. You see our oppression, You see our suffering, You see what we are going through, and You know who is responsible for this. It is not the devil, unless the devil lives in Pretoria now." And so we have said to God: "Just take them away." I did not pray for the state president's death; I simply prayed to God to give him another job – to send him into retirement.

Why are they afraid? First of all they say that you

cannot prescribe to God, because God will not listen to you then. And they know. But even with all their lies, even with all their untruthfulness, even with all their hypocrisy, they know that basically the truth is there. The God to whom we are praying is a God of justice, a God of liberation, and a God of freedom. He will come down, and He will deliver His people from the hand of the Pharaoh – whether he lives in Egypt or whether he lives in Groote Schuur or whether he lives in Pretoria. It will happen. And we know that they are therefore singing their last song. The time of this government is over. They are in their last death throe, and that is why they are doing what they are doing.

You know why they pay those ministers so very much money? They know that they are not going to be there for very long. And so what we are talking about is that we know that our struggle will not be in vain. What we are talking about is that we know that our struggle is just. What we are talking about is that we know that our people are not dying in vain. What we are talking about is that we know our children's blood is not being spilled in vain. What we are talking about is that we know that we have not struggled for all these years simply to sit in a hall and sing. We have struggled to be free; we have struggled so that the ideals enshrined in this Freedom Charter will become a reality.

And so, my brothers and sisters, I want to appeal to the people of this land, even at this late hour, to accept the demands and the ideals and the dream of the Freedom Charter. For the Freedom Charter in its very essence is the voice of the people of South Africa. If South Africa had only listened then in 1955, there would have been a democracy in this country. If South Africa had only listened then in 1955, detention without trial would have disappeared. Our people would never have been tortured in their jails, and Steve Biko and Reddy Sela and all the others would not have died at the hands of the police while they were in jail. If South Africa had listened, there would be no homelands. If South Africa had listened to the voice of its people in 1955, apartheid would have died long before it had become the monster that it is today.

If South Africa had only listened, there would have been far less violence in this country. The government would not have to depend on the army and the police and upon military violence to maintain its power, but the government would have had the love and the respect and the loyalty and the support of all its people.

If South Africa had only listened. If South Africa had only listened, Sharpeville would not have happened. If South Africa had listened to the voice of the people in the Freedom Charter, our children would not have died on the streets of Soweto in 1976. If South Africa had only listened, our people from Kwanobuhle and Langa would not have been killed here in Uitenhage. If South Africa had only listened, the massacre of Bloody Thursday would not have occurred. If South Africa had only listened to the voice of the people then, we would have had a better future.

And yet they have decided to ignore the voice of our people. So, my people, listen to me tonight: take the Freedom Charter and the demands and the dream of the Freedom Charter once again and make them your own. Base your future upon these basic foundations. It is not a faultless document, but it does enshrine the best that any country can offer its people in the world today. It is the only meaningful alternative to this evil system under which we must suffer so today. Therefore take these ideals. Make them your own. Take this dream and make it your own. Take this aspiration of our people in the Freedom Charter and make it your own. Take the ideals of the Freedom Charter and make them your own.

We do not need to become like the oppressor. The Freedom Charter has spelt out what the people of South Africa want to be. They do not need to become slaves of the violence of apartheid. The Freedom charter has spelt a better way. We do not need to remain slaves of a racist society. The Freedom Charter has spelt out a better way. We do not need to remain the slaves of capitalist exploitation. The Freedom Charter has spelt out a better way.

And so, let us come together. Let us seek the liberty that our people sought in 1955, and let us make that once again a unity in 1985. Let us move forward, knowing that the words of the Charter are the dream of our people. And let us say together tonight, for ourselves and for our children, that these are freedoms we will fight for side by side throughout our lives until we have won our liberty.

12

Raise a Sign of Hope

This is a funeral address delivered in Cradock on 20th July 1985 at the burial of Matthew Goniwe, Fort Calata, Sicelo Mhlawuli and Thomas Mkhonto, victims of the violence of that summer.

*

I have come to Cradock often in the past years. The first time was when Matthew Goniwe and Fort Calata were detained, and the people of Cradock asked me to come and visit with them, to come and see for myself what was happening in Lingilihle.

Since then I have learned to admire those men who have been such wonderful leaders in this community, and it has been a singular honour for me to work with them over the last year. I will not forget the last time I spoke in this very town of Cradock some five or six weeks ago. The people who came to listen were willing to wait from eight o'clock in the evening until I arrived at almost eleven o'clock. They did not move, which was a sign of the spirit that lived in Cradock. And that was a tribute to the leadership of the brothers whom we mourn today, and whom we will bury. When I think of their lives, when I think of what they have become – a symbol of our struggle, of our hope, of our determination, of our genius that we have in the black community in South Africa – and I think that we must bury them today, I must say so that all the world and this country can hear: If we have to bury men like Matthew Goniwe, men like our brothers Calata, Mkhonto and Mhlawuli, then this country is digging its own grave. South Africa is setting fire to its own future.

I am overcome by a terrible sadness and an anger, and I know that this sadness hangs all over our land. Because yet again, as so many times this year, we must mourn. Yet again we must bury our people. Yet again we must come and lay to rest some of the finest sons and daughters of our country. Yet again this government has shown that it will be utterly ruthless in its determination to hold on to power and to keep apartheid alive. Yet again we must say that something terrible is happening to this country. Look at where we are! Look at where we are! Apartheid, with its racism and its exploitation, is not only alive but is being defended with uncommon harshness. The Church is being persecuted for its obedience to God and for its decision to stand alongside the poor and the weak and the oppressed of our country.

There is unrest all over South Africa, for the cause of all the unrest and the violence has not yet been removed. The police and the army have laid siege to our townships. . . . The police and the army are conducting a reign of terror over our people. Our people disappear, we do not know what happens to them. Over the past few months more than ten thousand people have been detained and kept in jail. Thousands have been wounded, hundreds have been killed. Over the past few months there has been the emergence of death squads. I am not so sure that they are simply death squads put there by the so-called right-wing, for they have received too much protection over the last year. Our children die, like little Johannes Pochter the other day in Steytlerville, only twelve years old, beaten to death by the police. Our children die, as they have been dying for so many years now in those concentration camps in the resettlement areas, where there is no food and where there will be no nourishment from the moment they are born until the very week that they die, which will not be long after that.

This says to me that we must face up to the fact that in this government we are facing truly the spiritual children of Adolf Hitler. This is where we are. And today we are burying our brothers – who have not died by accident, nor is their death a mystery to us.

Our people who live here in the townships have testified, and they know what the truth is about these people and about the deaths of our brothers. Therefore we do not share those newspaper reports which talk about the mystery of the death of these four men. The United Democratic Front has raised certain issues and has asked certain fundamental questions about the death of Matthew Goniwe and Fort Calata and the other brothers. We have said publicly that only a very few people knew about the meeting that they were attending in Port Elizabeth, and that there was no public announcement as to when they would leave that night or whether they would come back to Cradock that evening. Only the people in the office knew that they were going to go back to Cradock that night, and the only other people who could have known were people who could listen in to that conversation with their sophisticated instruments. We know who they are.

We have been told that Matthew had said that evening that he would not stop the car unless he was stopped by uniformed police. We know that there was a roadblock that night. The question that must therefore be answered is: Who killed them? They were not struck down by lightning, the car did not mysteriously go up in flames. Our brothers were killed by the people who stopped them. Our people believe that the police did it – and I believe it too! It is time that we must say to this government: "Stop protecting these murderers who kill our people!" Who has been responsible for the systematic death of a number of our civic leaders over the past year, for they die mysteriously, they disappear mysteriously, they are being assassinated one after the other? Who is responsible for that?

And I want to say to the South African government, "Do *not* protect those people! Why have you created a climate in this country in which our children can be shot down in the streets by a policeman and that policeman can get away with it? Why have you created a climate in which death squads roam around and can do whatever they like as if the lives of our people do not matter? Why have you created a climate in which people know they can kill our leaders and they will not be brought to justice? Why have you created a climate in which the police can kill forty-three of our people without any provocation, and you set up a commission of enquiry, and still the police will be held blameless?" I must say to the South African government, "We have said to you before and we are saying to you again: there is a God in heaven who knows about justice, and you shall reap what you sow!"

And yet while this is happening, it seems that most of our white brothers and sisters in this country cannot be bothered. They are more concerned about the cancellation of a rugby tour than they are about the lives of our people! I have seen more concern in our newspapers for the "All Blacks" who are not coming to South Africa than for our people who have died. In most of white South Africa, they are calling for stronger tactics by the government. Most refuse to hear the truth, most refuse to listen to the voice of the oppressed and of our people who suffer. They would rather listen to the propaganda on South African television than they would to the voice of Mrs Goniwe, who will tell them about her husband and what he did and the work he had done for the sake not only of our people but for all of South Africa. While we are suffering, and while we are crying out, white South Africa mostly wants to make heroes out of those black people who are willing to sell their souls for money and the little bit of political power that P. W. Botha will give them . . .

I must say to our white brothers and sisters, I am so grateful that some of you are here today to show your solidarity. I hope that you will go away from this funeral today with more than merely sympathy in your hearts, because we do not need that. We need your total commitment to the struggle; we need your joining in the struggle; we need your voices to be heard; we need your bodies in the struggle. And so we hope that you will go and use the power that you have, so you can go and tell the government that this evil system must be eradicated. You can go and you can tell the government that they must stop killing our people. I hope that you will use the opportunities you have to do just that, and thereby forge links of brotherhood and sisterhood that cannot be broken even by the evil of racism or by the propaganda of the South African government.

I would plead with white South Africa, please do not be deceived by what you hear and see and by those who so cunningly can twist the truth even by quoting the Bible. The state president spoke a week ago to hundreds of young white people. He said to them that it is his duty to stop terrorism, just as Jesus drove out the money changers from the temple. I would like to ask the state president whether he knows what he is doing when he tries to read a theology of violence into the life of the man whom the Bible calls the Prince of Peace. I would like to know why those church leaders who are so quick to condemn us when we ask to pray for the removal of unjust rule and who say that we want violence − why don't they rise up and tell the state president: "You cannot use the name of Jesus to justify your violence"? Why are they silent? It is their duty to preach not only to those people who are voiceless but it is even more their duty to preach to those who have the power to change this country tomorrow if they want to.

And another thing: the state president must think about whether he is right in simply assuming that the terrorists he is talking about are those brothers who have to fight from across the border. The experience of black people in this country is different. We do not think that the terrorists are those who are the freedom fighters of this land. The African National Congress (ANC) did not shoot our people when they were defenceless at Sharpeville twenty-five years ago. The ANC did not kill our children in 1976 when they were walking peacefully on the streets of Soweto. The ANC did not kill our children during the school boycotts in 1980 in Cape Town. It was not the ANC who killed little Thabo Sibeko, who was six years old, last year on the East Rand. It was not the ANC who killed forty-three people at Langa township on 21st March at the massacre of Uitenhage. It was not the ANC who killed our four brothers whom we are burying today. The government did it – and so *they* are the terrorists! It is a most dangerous thing when people in power begin to believe their own propaganda!

And I urge those white people who are serious about the future of South Africa: look a little further than your newspapers, listen a little deeper than to the voices of the commentators on South African television, and come and talk to our people in the townships. There you will hear the truth. There you will see the truth. There you will see what it means to live under apartheid. I know that this funeral will not be the last one. I know that our mourning will not end today. I know that tomorrow and tomorrow and tomorrow and tomorrow there will be more tears that will flow. And there are difficult days ahead. The violence of the South African government knows no end. More of our brothers and sisters will be detained. There will be more whose names will be added to some hit list, and more will be killed by those faceless murderers who hide behind balaclavas and who hide behind their guns and who hide behind the protection that they get.

But this is the price that we have to pay for our freedom. We are here today, but we will do more than just mourn. We have heard it over and over again. We will not simply mourn; we will wake up from mourning, and we will dedicate ourselves anew to the struggle for justice and liberation and freedom and peace.

If I die tomorrow, do not come to my funeral and sing freedom songs if you are not willing to participate today in the struggle for liberation and justice. If I die tomorrow, do not revenge my death with more senseless violence and hatred, but raise up a sign of hope that this country will become what it must become and that we will make our contribution to that. If I die tomorrow, do not give up and do not despair, for I know that our victory is near, and that apartheid and injustice will never endure and that our people shall be free. If I die tomorrow, raise up a sign that the victory of this country is not written in the guns and the violence, and the armies of the South African government, but that the victory and the future of this country are written in the hearts of our people in our determination to be free and in our willingness to give our lives for the struggle that we believe in.

I know that as we have to go from funeral to funeral many of us will become tired. Many of us will become tired of protest, will become tired of knocking at the door, will become tired of seeing our brothers and sisters dying so much. But as long as our people, black and white, are shackled in the chains of oppression and racism, there will be a fight to fight, and we must not give up. As long as our children die needlessly and untimely there will be a fight to fight – do not give up. And as long as injustice still reigns supreme in this land there will be a fight to fight – do not give up. As long as little children are born just to die, too soon, there will be a fight to fight – do not give up. For this country is yours, this land is yours, the future is yours – do not give it up.

So while we mourn, let us commit ourselves again to the struggle for justice and freedom and liberation. There are things that we can do. We can begin to ask ourselves what those of us who come from Natal, and those of us who come from the Western Cape, and those of us who come from Transvaal, should ask ourselves: Why it is that the people in the Eastern

Cape can have a successful consumer boycott, but we do not do anything about that in the Cape or Natal or Transvaal! One of the things that should come out of this funeral is for the people of this country to go back home and organize for that, and we will lay low those who think they are the powerful. We will keep away from them our buying power. We should begin to do that. We must do it in Cape Town, we must do it in Johannesburg, and we must do it in Durban.

And to our people in the townships who have shops I say, You are part of this struggle too. When we say that we shall boycott the white shops we want your full co-operation. We want you to make it possible for our people to do that. You do not raise your prices, you lower them. You lower them because it is the cause of the struggle. And if you do that you will be known as people who fight with us and who struggle with us for justice.

I must say that if the only thing we do when we go back home is to raise a sign of hope for our people so that we can see, and the world can see, that in spite of what is happening to us we are not a defeated people, we shall have achieved a noble purpose.

13

If You Believe

This was the first sermon preached by Allan Boesak after his release from three weeks of solitary confinement. He delivered it to his own Bellville congregation on 22nd September 1985.

*

My brothers and sisters, I came upon this text exactly a week ago, while I was in my cell in Pretoria Central Prison, after one of the most difficult weekends in all my life. The first two weeks I could bear. Even the silence, even not being able to speak with anyone, not being able to open my heart, not being able to share my feelings, my fears, my anxieties, or my longings. Not being able to tell anyone how much I missed my wife and my children, my family, my congregation. It was only in those days that I discovered how much I love this congregation in Bellville and how much all of you have become part of my heart and of my life and why it is that God, through very difficult days – and you know those days – has kept me in this congregation for nine years now.

But the third week became almost too much for me. By 3 o'clock in the afternoon they bring your supper. By 3.30 they lock up and slam the grille in your cell and double-lock it. They slam the steel door and double-lock that too, and finally the two grilles in the passage.

That Friday afternoon of the third week was no different. As I sat silently in my cell, the noises of the wardens leaving the prison building faded away, and on the floor above me I could hear the other prisoners talking with one another, reading the newspapers of the day, discussing, sometimes laughing – and I had no one to share this with. No one to talk to.

I had been on my knees almost constantly for three weeks, praying to God to lead me out of that darkness and out of that pain and out of that suffering. And nothing happened. Then the moment came when I fell on my knees and I cried as I never cried before. Maybe for the first time since I was a little boy. I then said to God, "I do not understand this. Why have You brought me here? It's been three weeks now, God, and I have prayed every day and I have tried to believe that You in Your power will take me out of this place of imprisonment and bring me out into the world again, to the community of the living again." For when you are locked up like that you sometimes feel as good as dead.

For three weeks I have believed that somehow God would work through the international community to put pressure on the South African government to let me out. After three weeks, that did not happen. All my life I have tried to hold on to my faith. I have preached the Gospel as honestly as I could because I believe that Jesus has called me to do that. I said to God, "Why, if I am Your servant, if I have tried to do what is right in this world, have You done this to me? I have said it all. You know, God, what happened to me in this year, in 1985. Wasn't that enough? Why must I now sit here in this prison, not understanding, not seeing any way out of this?" I wrestled with God. I fought with God. I said to Him, "I was a fool! If I were a little more clever, I would have accepted those positions that were offered

me in America, to become a professor of theology at a
world-renowned university. I could have pursued the
nomination to become the General Secretary of the
World Council of Churches. I could at least have asked
my supporters, yes, please lobby for me. Instead, I
wrote to the search committee and said no, I do not
want this position because I believe that my place, at
this time in history, is in South Africa. If I were wise, I
could have taken my wife and children and left South
Africa, because I know what happens to people in this
land who try to struggle for justice and for peace. If I
had done this," I said to God, "my wife and my
children would have been with me. If I had done this, I
would have been safe now. If I had done this, I would
not have been in this place now." I said to God, "You
made me believe that the struggle for justice and
human dignity, the struggle for peace and humanity in
South Africa is also *Your* struggle. You made me
believe, from the very beginning, that my opposition
to the South African government was never of my
own. It was an opposition that was based always upon
my faith in Jesus Christ and upon the certain
knowledge that apartheid is a heresy and that it cannot
be defended on the basis of the Gospel. I believed that
my involvement in the political struggle for the sake of
the weak and the poor and the needy is an integral part
of my discipleship, is the heart of my discipleship in
this country. This is what You, God, have called me to
do. Why have You made me believe this and yet
brought me to this place?"

That was the most difficult moment of my life. As I
was there on my knees, the words couldn't come any
more and there were no more tears to cry. Friday night
went by and Saturday morning dawned and there was
still no answer. Saturday night came, and I wrestled

through the night and still I found no answer. My difficulty with this God whom we cannot see, whom we have to believe in although He will not break through the prison walls and make His voice plain to me so that I could hear another voice apart from my own to reassure me, became unbearable. I thought to myself: I have always preached from this pulpit (and you are my witnesses!) that I believe in the power of God. That Jesus Christ is Lord and King and that therefore no government on earth can detain the power of God. But as I sat there in that jail, and as the days and the nights crawled by and that weekend dawned upon me and I still could see only darkness, I said to myself, "Am I to believe that the power of P. W. Botha and the Minister for Law and Order is greater than the power of this almighty God?"

But on Sunday morning I opened my Bible to read. I am not one of those who believe that you just open the Bible and mysteriously God will show you a passage. But I opened my Bible to find a word of consolation, a word of light, a word of inspiration, a word of truth that would take away from me my uncertainty, my fear, my anxiety — a word that I could hold on to. And without my having looked for it, my Bible fell open at the Gospel of Mark, chapter 9, and like the blast of a trumpet the words of Jesus fell on my ears: "If you believe, all things are possible to those who believe." And then I knew. That night, Sunday, 15th September, I sat down and wrote a letter to my wife and said to her, "I have wrestled with God and it is over. I now know that I will be with you before the weekend."

In this passage I saw my own dilemma as I came to understand the dilemma of this father who brought his sick child to Jesus. The dilemma of this father begins with the fact that his child was ill. Today we would say that this child was an epileptic. All the symptoms were there. But in those days they did not know this. They only saw something they did not understand, that threatened their existence, their lives, and the meaning and worth of their lives. And when they experienced something that threatened the good order of God as God meant it to be, the only way they could express their feelings of fear was to say: "This is an evil spirit." They understood their struggle as not so much against the illness, but as a struggle against the spirit of evil that had seized this boy, that had this boy in its grip, that would not let go, that would kill this boy. "Sometimes," the father said to Jesus, "the spirit will grab him and throw him in the water, and sometimes in the fire." He might burn to death at any moment; he might drown at any moment. What was he to do?

The issue here is not merely their inadequate understanding or our knowledge of illness based on modern scientific methods and research. Neither is it a question of our superiority, since we no longer speak of "evil spirits" when someone is ill. There is something more to this. We like to believe that through our scientific know-how we have conquered all. We make believe that we can control everything – including life and death. We have conquered the world and we have enslaved nature. We colonize the heavens, and we plant our silly little flags and nationalistic symbols on the planets and the stars. We take giant steps for humankind, or so we claim, and we wait for God to crawl back into His corner and leave the world to be run by those who through their knowledge and power can do it – namely us. But we cannot face the reality of evil, either in our world or in ourselves. Yes, we conquer space and we win battles against killer germs. Yet at the same time we are destroying the world and we *create* killer germs and nuclear arms, enough to destroy not only *this* world but also worlds yet undiscovered. We want to create life while we still have not learned to respect life. The same governments who claim to be the protectors of the unborn child dish out medals of honour to the soldier who kills more efficiently than the "enemy". But we ignore or deny these contradictions because we do not want to face the reality of evil.

The Gospel wants to tell us very clearly that evil is real. Let us make no mistake. Evil in this world is real, it is tangible; you can see it, you can taste it, you can feel it, you can experience it. For anything, anything at all that goes against the will of God, anything that threatens our human existence, anything that destroys humanity, anything that is violent, or destructive, or inhuman, is evil, and that evil is real. That is something we so-called modern people have lost sight of. So we have no reason to say, "Oh, in those times they were primitive. They did not understand as we understand; it is out of ignorance that they spoke of evil spirits." No, people of God, no, even today we must understand that evil is real. And evil spirits in this world are real. Anything that goes against the will of God for this world, that tries to destroy the vision that God has for this world – of peace and justice, of human dignity and wholeness, of life and love of the community – that is evil and it is real. That is why it makes sense that the Apostle Paul writes:

For we are not contending against flesh and blood, but against the principalities, against the powers, against the world rulers of this present darkness, against the spiritual hosts of wickedness in the heavenly places. Ephesians 6:12

This is true. When we confront the utter callousness of people who will do anything at all, destroy anyone at all, simply to hold on to power, then you must understand that evil is real. We are facing a government that will allow children to die of hunger, that will allow people to be shot on the street as if their lives do not matter. When this happens, you must know that evil is real. And when lawlessness dresses up as law, and when inhumanity and brutality pose as law and order, when injustice claims to be justice and when the heresy of apartheid is defended as Christian, evil is real. Christian churches send telegrams when we plan peaceful protests against this government, because our resistance threatens their vested interests. But when we are thrown in jail under a law that should not even have existed, that is a travesty of justice, a denial of every basic human right, they keep quiet. When our people are terrorized, when the police and the army make war against our defenceless children, when pregnant women and our old people are beaten with sjamboks and brutally assaulted in their own homes, they are quiet. When our young people are shot to death for daring to resist, they do not speak or send telegrams of protest. No, they are as quiet as the graves our children lie in. When this happens, evil is real.

And let us not say that evil spirits existed only in the times of Jesus when people were "primitive". No, my brothers and sisters, evil exists in this country, even now. Evil dresses itself up in black ties and black suits and top hats, and sits in parliament and makes the laws that undermine the dignity of the people of South Africa. Evil sits in parliament and defends the cold-blooded murder of our leaders. Evil stands in the pulpit and justifies the oppression and ongoing violence of apartheid. Evil sits in padded chairs in air-conditioned boardrooms, continues the financing of apartheid, and self-righteously claims it is protecting the poor. And in the meantime the prophets of God are silenced, not because we want to kill or destroy or hate, but because we preach a message of peace, love and justice. We are thrown in jail because that message of truth is too much to bear for those who live on untruths.

I have not given up my conviction for our nonviolent struggle for justice in this country. If it is God's will, it is God's struggle – and I will continue to do that for as long as God gives me breath in my body. I want to say to my people: Do not give up this struggle. We must not turn to violence, because violence will destroy us as much as it has destroyed the people who are using it against us. Violence will destroy our soul even as their violence has destroyed their souls. They have no wisdom left, they have no understanding, they have no insight. They have no God left except the god of their guns, their casspirs, their tanks, and their weapons of destruction. Let them pray to that god. Our God is the living God – the God of justice and freedom. To this God we will pray. To His service we will dedicate ourselves.

And so, my people, understand that our struggle is against the evil spirits of this world. Let us remain with Jesus. Let us remain with the Spirit of God in our hearts. Let us depend on His power. Not on the power of guns or the destruction of life. That will be my message to you always. Let us seek the peace which only God Himself will give us in this country, even though they who rule so harshly may not understand it. Even today I do not hate them. I will not hate them, but I will resist them until the very end, because I love this country and I love them and I love my people too much to allow the oppressors to destroy us. This we must know.

In our gospel story, the father of the sick boy came to

Jesus and explained his dilemma. At the same time, his dilemma became the dilemma of Jesus's disciples, because they could not heal this boy. It was painful. After all, they knew Jesus best, walked with him, heard his voice, understood him better than anyone else. They heard his teachings. And yet they were not able to heal the boy. That was *their* dilemma; a dilemma which became an embarrassment not only before the father, but especially also before the scribes and Pharisees. As our story begins, there was an argument between the scribes and Pharisees and the disciples of Jesus, because the disciples could not heal the boy. They seemed helpless. They had heard Jesus say that if you have faith, you will tell this mountain to move itself from here into the sea. Why couldn't they do it now? They had heard Jesus say that if you have faith even like a mustard seed you will tell this tree to uproot itself and remove itself to another place. Why couldn't they do that? This was their dilemma.

But as Jesus arrives the real nature of the dilemma is revealed. Jesus comes and tells them: "Oh faithless people, how long shall I be with you?" And that, in essence, is the real dilemma of the father and the disciples: their faithlessness, their inability to believe. Jesus says, "All things are possible for those who believe." I smiled a little cynically when I read that the first time. I thought: "God, if this is true, why am I still in this prison? If this is true, why is this government still in power? If this is true, why can they roam our streets and shoot our people while there is nothing we can do about it? If this is true, how is it possible that the Church of Jesus Christ cannot stand together? That even in the Church we are still divided? Why is it that some in the Church are willing to sell our brothers and sisters for the sake of position or out of fear or for love of money? Why? How can I believe that if we only believe *all things* are possible – even the removal of this evil government?" That is possible, if you believe, Jesus says.

But the problem lies not with Jesus, nor with God, nor with the promises of God. The problem lies with us, with you and with me. We are the problem. And in this respect the problem is not even the government of this country with all its power, because God can remove them. . . . But the promises of God are clear. We must learn not to be intimidated by the so-called "realities" of our world. Right through the Bible the promises of God are there. "Abraham," said God, "you will have a son. Even though you are so old, you will have a son." And Abraham and Sarah did have a son, for the promises of God endure. Joseph dreams. God promises him in that dream: "I will lift you up, even though you do not count among your brothers, and I will make you one to whom even they will look for help." Joseph is sold by his brothers as a slave. Joseph is thrown in jail by Potiphar and it seems that all is lost. Yet somehow the promises of God remain true, and Joseph is raised up to become the symbol of God's providence not only for Egypt but for the whole world. Mary hears the promise of God that the Messiah will be born and God's new day will dawn. The high and the mighty will be thrown from their thrones. The rich will be sent away empty and the poor will be lifted up from the dust of the earth. The humble will be lifted up and placed in high places by God, and the hungry will be filled with good things. This is the promise of God.

I heard and I believed. I learned to depend, not on Allan Boesak who can talk and argue his way out of anything, but on the promises of God alone. I was humbled before God for almost four weeks. Twenty-five days of solitary confinement, spent in prayer, sometimes fasting, have taught me to depend on the Spirit of God alone, and that the Word of God is true. And as this Word from the Gospel came to me then, I said to God: "You will lead me out of here, You will change my situation, You will change this land, You will bring our people our freedom, You will give our people back our dignity, You will give our people vision, You will give our people Your love, You will give our people their land, You will give our people the strength to stand, and to believe and to fight, *if I believe*. If I believe, all things are possible."

Today I am here, back in this pulpit, not because of *my* faith but because the God of heaven and earth is alive. And I say to you, my people, my own congregation, we have gone through so many difficult times this year, but God has brought us closer together. Keep that love in your hearts. Keep each other in love and in communion of spirit and in communion of commitment. Let the congregation of Bellville become a light and a symbol of love and commitment to Jesus Christ, of love and commitment to the world. Let this church become a symbol of how Christians in this country must participate in this struggle for the sake of Jesus Christ, and also for the sake of justice and peace. Be an example to the Dutch Reformed Mission Church, even to your Moderator. Be an example to every single church. Be an example to every organization. Let the light of Jesus become alive in this congregation, not for our own sakes but for the sake of him who died for us and for the sake of the truth, for the sake of justice, for the sake of peace. Let us challenge the tensions within ourselves. Let us not become cynical. Let us not become hopeless. Let us believe in a committed, faithful, peaceful community.

Let us see visions of love and peace and harmony and dignity and liberation for our country, for *all* the people. And all things are possible for those who believe. To believe is to stand up and be counted for Jesus and for justice. To believe is to stand up and to work for justice. To believe is to be willing to take the risks knowing that God is on your side.

I can tell you this now with more conviction than ever before: He who believes, she who believes, and works for justice and for peace will never be alone. You will never be alone because Jesus promised that whatever happens, he will never leave us alone – even in the darkness of a cell in solitary confinement. So let us believe and not despair. Let us believe and work for justice. Let us believe and seek peace. Let us believe and challenge evil in this world. Let us believe and build together a community of love and joy and power and liberation.

There is one last word. If you believe, you can make this your own. Dietrich Bonhoeffer, that courageous German theologian who had so much influence on my life, as much as Martin Luther King had, was killed by the Nazis because of his resistance to their evil. A few weeks before Germany was freed by the allied forces the Germans hanged him. He was only thirty-nine years old. I loved that man, and I love his testimony and praise God for him. In January 1935 Bonhoeffer wrote to his brother and said: "There are things in this world which are worth fighting for without any compromise whatsoever. And it seems to me that peace and social justice, which is really Jesus Christ, is such a cause." That is my belief. My people, believe in Jesus Christ and make this your conviction. That is what I told the major when I had read that piece. I told him that again on Thursday when I was told I would be released. I say this to you this morning, and to those of the security police who are monitoring this sermon. There are things in this world which are worth standing up for and fighting for without compromise: peace and justice, which is really Jesus Christ.

I believe in Jesus.
I believe in justice.
I believe in peace.
I believe in liberation.
I believe in God's vision for this country.

I believe, also, that it will come true, for Jesus is saying it again to me and to you. Don't worry about my detention or my bail conditions. Don't worry about my trial. God will take care of all of us. I do not worry. I sleep well at night. My life is in the hands of God. God will take care of us. You, you must commit yourselves anew.

Believe in Jesus.
Believe in Jesus and fight for what is right.
God bless you all! Amen.

14

The Price is High,
but the End is Near

Allan Boesak preached this sermon on 6th October
1985, at a prayer service for political detainees, shortly
after his own release from detention.

*

Oh Lord, how many are my foes. Many are rising against
me. Many are saying of me, there is no help for him in
God. But Thou, O Lord, are the shield about me, my glory
and the lustre of my head. I cry aloud to the Lord, and He
answers me from His holy hill. I lie down and sleep; I
wake again, for the Lord sustains me. I am not afraid of ten
thousands of people who have set themselves against me
round about. Arise, O Lord, deliver me, O my God, for
Thou dost smite all my enemies on the cheek; Thou dost
break the teeth of the wicked. Deliverance belongs to the
Lord. Thy blessing be upon Thy people.

Psalm 3

Those men who put us in jail and who question us and
who think up charges in the middle of the night
because sleep has fled from their eyes – they cannot
sleep. Their consciences bother them because they
know that time is up, and while they cannot sleep they
think of charges to put down on paper, and they take us
to court in communities across the land. And because
they know that they really cannot ban us, because that

would look too bad, they make up a banning order in the form of bail conditions and they impose that upon us. And they think that now the voice of justice, the voice of peace, and the voice for liberation has been silenced.

It is not my voice that they are trying to silence. They are trying to silence the voice of the Almighty God – and that is not possible. Justice does not belong to human beings to do with what we like. Justice belongs to God, and God gives that justice to a people to be the basis of our struggle, to be the vision into our future, to be the sustenance as the road gets long and difficult and as we get weary. Only God can take that vision away. Only God can take that sustenance away. It is not in the power of a government to take that away from a struggling people. That they must understand.

The government doesn't even have power to give or to share. Mr P. W. Botha said, "The government is willing to share its power." With whom? What power do they have to share? Jesus Christ said a long time ago as he stood before Pontius Pilate, "You would have no power over me were it not given you from above." So I say to P. W. Botha and I say to all of those henchmen of Satan who think that they rule this land: "You would have no power over us were it not given you from above. And God has given us a clear sign in this land that power is being taken away from you because you do not deserve it. You have misused it."

But there is something else that I want you to understand as we meditate upon a question of our own situation and the struggle. Psalm 3 is a psalm that David wrote while he was on the run from his son Absalom. Absalom was planning a military coup. He sat at the gate of the city, speaking to all who would come by, trying to explain to them that he would be a much better king than David. The danger of the situation for David was clear. We know that in the end he had to flee from Jerusalem across the River Jordan to hide away from his own child. The danger was clear, the situation was serious because it was not only David in his person who was endangered. The reign of David, the throne of David, symbolized something – it represented God's justice in the world and for Israel. David was the kind of king that God wanted to use as His example of the kind of reign that the Messiah would have in the world. And so what Absalom was trying to undermine was not merely the throne of his father, but the dream of God – justice, love, peace, compassion and understanding.

So David says twice in the first two verses, "Many are rising up against me; my enemies are too much for me to count." This story is also recounted in the Second Book of Samuel, chapter 15, where it says that the hearts of the men of Israel were drawn toward Absalom. Verse 2 in the psalm is a cry of pain and anguish from a troubled heart. David says that many are saying of him, "No help is coming to him from God. God has left him in the lurch; God has left him alone. He looks around and there is no one to support him. The power of his enemies is too much for him." It seems in that situation as if even God is not only silent but also powerless over against the power of Absalom and his plans. But then David looks at God and he says, "My faith shall remain. I will be certain that God will help. God shall rise up and save me. Thou dost smite my enemies in the face."

In Second Samuel we hear that the armies of David go out, they fight against Absalom, Absalom's armies are defeated, and Absalom himself is killed. When David hears the news he goes up into his room, and he refuses to eat. He refuses to drink. He refuses to rejoice. He sees no reason to celebrate his liberation. He has come back from exile, he has crossed the Jordan River once again, he is once again enthroned in Jerusalem. But he is unhappy, and he mourns the death of his son. He grieves so much that the soldiers become restless and even a little ashamed until Joab comes and speaks to him and says, "How can you do this? These men have been willing to give up their lives for you. They have left their wives and their children for you. They have left their homes for you. They have risked everything for you. God has given you victory over your enemies. You have prayed for this victory. Now that God has granted your prayer, what are you doing? You mourn because you now begin to understand that the price of liberation is costly." Then David realizes this is the truth, and he comes out and speaks to his men.

The point that I want to make today is precisely this. It is not necessary for me to tell you what is happening in our country, for you know that. It is not necessary for me to explain to you what the nature of our struggle for justice and peace and liberation is, for you know that. It is not necessary for me to explain to you what your calling is, how clear you must be in your own minds, for you know that. Many of you have participated, are participating, in this struggle. Too many of us are still standing on the sidelines, wondering whether we should come in or not; whether it will be safe or not; worrying about our own safety; worrying about our jobs; worrying about I don't know who. Many of us have joined this struggle, and that is important.

But we must know that there is a price that we must pay for liberation. This is no joke, this thing that we

are engaged in. When people are no longer sure
whether they will be there tomorrow, it is no joke.
When our children's education is being disrupted, it is
no joke. When mothers and fathers do not know
whether they will see their children together around
the table tonight as they saw them last night and the
day before, it is no joke. And when our townships are
being overrun by troop-carriers and tank-like vehicles
and soldiers with guns and live ammunition, it is no
joke. And when people are being beaten up and there is
no respect for little children or for pregnant women or
for our fathers and mothers who have come along in
age, this is no joke.

But as this happened, and as the months went on and
on, and as the death toll rose, and as many more were
picked up and detained, locked up in their jails, and as
many more had to go underground in hiding so that
they could not continue the work that the people have
entrusted them to do – as this was happening, and as it
seemed as if all of what we were trying to do could not
keep the guns away from us and the dogs and the whips
and the quirts and the tear gas – as this was happening,
many of us started doubting. We asked the questions:
What now? Is this really worth it? When will it end?
Wasn't this enough? Yes, yes, yes, we are willing to
sacrifice, but how much more? I am saying to you who
have those feelings in your heart, you are like David.
Because as the moment of liberation comes near, so
the price that we have to pay for that liberation will
become higher and higher and higher.

We are not dealing with some benevolent government who understands justice and mercy and
freedom and liberation and compassion. We are not
dealing with people who understand the struggle of a
people to be free. We are not dealing with people who

understand the meaning of the word "dignity". We are dealing with people who have closed off their hearts and their minds and their ears so that they cannot hear the voice of God any more. We are dealing with people whose hearts have so been hardened that they cannot understand the will of God for this country any more. I have said so in the past, and I will say so again: in this government we are not dealing with the servant of God, we are dealing with the beast from the sea. That is what we are dealing with, and you had better be clear about it.

And as for those men who call themselves Christians, we are not dealing with Christians. We are dealing with people who have long since forgotten what it means to open this Word of God and to hear the voice of God as it speaks to them. That is who we are dealing with.

The price we will have to pay is not paid yet. The struggle is not over yet. As I sat in that jail for twenty-five days in solitary confinement and thought at one point I would go out of my mind, I knew that this was not yet the end. There will be many more such moments, either for me or for others. Many more of our people will have to lose their jobs because of their commitment to the struggle for justice. There will be many more like that. There will be many more of our children who will not be able to go to school because of the crisis to which this government has brought us.

Don't let anybody tell you that this crisis was brought upon us either by our children or by our teachers or by the workers or by the UDF or by the trade union. Those are the lies and the propaganda without which no unjust government can survive. They have to use them; otherwise they cannot live. But the chaos in this country is the result of the policy of a government which is unjust, cruel, inhuman, un-Christian. It has no relation at all to human dignity and decency. This you must understand. And as long as this government is in power, parents, your children will be in a situation of chaos. As long as this government is in power our society will be in chaos. As long as this government is in power our land will be in chaos.

And so as we fight against this system, remember: the struggle will be long and hard. As we pay the price, don't look around. Don't say, I have had enough; I have prayed enough. Don't say, I have struggled enough. Don't say, I have suffered enough. As long as the blood on the streets which has flowed from the bodies of our children is not dry, that blood will call to God in heaven and to you. Don't close your eyes. Don't close your ears. Don't close your heart. It may very well be that this government will continue to repress us, and I fully expect that it will happen – the repression will grow. The . . . and the P. W. Bothas of this world will say what they say and do what they do more and more, because the more we struggle and victory comes closer, the more the world sees them for what they are. The more we rise up with dignity and power to challenge the unjust powers, the more they will have to shout, the more they will have to shoot, the more they will have to kill. It is true; they will do that. Apartheid is like that god Molech that lived on the sacrifice of little children in the ancient days. As long as that beast is alive, we will have to make sacrifices.

But we are seeing the final convulsion of that beast. And as David learned, you must learn: there is no easy way to freedom. There is no golden road to freedom. There is no rosy road to freedom – forget about that. Our calling is clear. Our goal is clear. The struggle must continue at every level because the end is near. The South African government knows – but I will say it to them again today so that they will understand it and you must know it – their end is near.

And so we will remain faithful to God, faithful to our calling, faithful to our faith. We will pay the price, but the end is near. We hear the voices of anguish and pain. We hear them, and the price is high, but the end is near. We see the suffering of mothers and fathers and children, and the price is high, but the end is near. We see the disruption of our communities and we see the chaos in which we live, and the price is high, but the end is near. We see the tears on the cheeks of those who have buried loved ones who have died in the struggle, and we share their grief. And we know the price is high, but the end is near. We see at this moment justice still stumbling on the streets of South Africa, and apartheid still reigning supreme on the throne of this land, and the price is high, but the end is near. We hear the voice of the police as it shouts at us, as it tries to frighten us, as it tries to intimidate us, and we know the price is high, but the end is near.

We know, we know that we will have to pay, and it is costly. And the struggle is long and hard, and the road is arduous. The price is high, but the end is near. Do not despair. Do not look around. Do not betray our faith. Do not betray our children. Do not betray our fathers. Do not betray our mothers. Do not betray our vision. Do not betray the justice we are fighting for. Do not betray the land. We will see that it will rise up out of the ashes of this country as apartheid will crumble to dust. The price will be high, but the end is near.

15

I Have Seen Satan Fall

16th June 1986 marked the tenth anniversary of the Soweto uprising. The ceremonies and demonstrations commemorating that day were the focus of international attention, and at their centre was this sermon Allan Boesak preached at a memorial service in Cape Town.

*

My dear brothers and sisters, there are very few people assembled from the townships here this morning, and we know why. As we continue our service let us pray to God that He will protect our brothers and sisters who were on their way to this service, and who in all probability have been stopped this morning by the police at roadblocks. We do not know what is happening to them, but in the midst of all that terror may God be with them and may God protect them.

I must say something else before I begin my sermon. You have all seen in the newspapers the explanation of what the state of emergency means. You also may have seen the definition of what is called subversion. I am already in a court case, having been accused of subversion. If you have read that definition clearly you understand that it actually means that anything you say that somehow criticizes the government, or that criticizes the actions of the Minister for Law and

Order, or that criticizes the actions of his police and army, or anything that can be understood by him to be subversive – that is an offence, punishable by law.

Now you know me – I'm not a very brave person. . . . When you are called to preach the Gospel of Jesus Christ you cannot turn around and search out what the government finds acceptable. You will have to say what God wants you to say, and that Word shall be for ever the last Word. No one gladly confronts this evil government. No one gladly goes to jail – I've been there and know what it's like. But if for the preaching of this Word I have to go again, then so be it.

*

So this morning we have chosen for our text what you read in Luke, chapter 10, verse 18: "And Jesus said to them, 'I saw Satan fall like lightning from heaven.'"

We are here to commemorate Soweto 1976, to think again upon that most solemn moment in our history. We know what 16th June means for us. It means that after almost a generation of passivity, it was our children who rose up and said "No" to apartheid, to continued exploitation, to inferior and unequal education; "No" to racism and oppression. And at the same time they said "Yes" to dignity, freedom and the future for all the children of this land. We know that Soweto is more than just a name. It is more than just a symbol. We know that Soweto has become the perpetual condition of South Africa. We know that the words from Shakespeare's play *Macbeth* have become so true for our country during this time: "Alas, for a country almost afraid to know itself; it cannot be called our mother, but our grave." South Africa has become a grave for the hopes of millions of oppressed people. It has become the grave for the dreams of our children, their dreams of freedom and hope and joy. It has become to a large extent the grave of the authenticity of the Gospel of Jesus Christ, that Gospel that has been so evilly abused by those in power who call themselves Christians, while every single act they commit is a denial of this God they claim to know and serve. It has become the grave of the dreams of those of us who hold on to dignity and to life and to a future.

During Soweto 1976 our people for ever lost their innocence. We then saw our children going into the streets with nothing in their hands but placards calling for the removal of Afrikaans – such a simple, simple issue – from their curriculum. That's how it began. They went into the streets, when others were detained, saying, We do not want to make war, we simply want you to release our friends. And later on we saw them on the street battling the police armed with R-1 rifles, they with nothing in their hands, singing freedom songs and dying on the streets. We then saw how Hector Peterson was killed, the first boy to die in that new era of violence and oppression and hatred and cruelty. We saw the extent to which the South African government is willing to go in order to defend white privilege and their own position of power. We saw then that they are willing to kill our children by the hundreds, only so that they can cling to power. We saw then that violence was going to be the language of the South African government from that time on – as it had been before, but even more so from that moment. We then knew what it is, finally and clearly, that we are dealing with.

Now they have again, for the second time in one year, declared a state of emergency. They have banned all these commemorations. They first tried to ban our church services, but when the Church of Jesus Christ said very clearly, "You can try to ban these services; we will continue anyway," then they had to back-pedal on that one. And yet yesterday they arrested a whole churchful of people at St Nicholas. They broke up the service with tear gas, and policemen with guns took them away, the women to one jail, the men elsewhere – even children gone with their mothers. Fourteen days they will be locked up. Their crime: having come together on a Sunday afternoon in a parish church to listen to the Word of God and to pray.

They do this because they want to force us to forget 16th June 1976. They want to force us to forget the history of this country, the history of our struggle. They have robbed us of our land. They have oppressed our people. They have raped our country. They have undermined our faith. They have vilified and exiled and jailed and killed our leaders. They have terrorized our people in our communities. They have massacred our children. And now they want us to forget. We shall never forget. We shall never annul this part of our history, simply let it fade away or be forced out of our minds because they want us to be so fearful of them that we become a people without a past. The government knew too well that our commemoration would be once again a national demonstration of our rejection of its policies, of its force, of its undemocratic rule, of its very legitimacy. They knew that. And we are here not because in the first place we are looking for confrontation, as they so glibly lie on their television. We are here not because we want to die, but we are here because we refuse to let our fear become the grave of our dignity. And it is time that the South African government understands that.

How can we forget 16th June? How can we forget

what we have seen since then, because since then, 16th June, Soweto has been enacted over and over and over again in our country's history. The story of Hector Peterson and all those other children has been multiplied a thousandfold, in Soweto and in townships right across South Africa. You know that. Since then we have heard the horrifying story of the efforts of this government completely to obliterate from the face of this country the presence of our people, or at least the kind of presence that we want to be, namely, a dignified, protesting, hopeful, accusing presence. As long as we are here and as long as we rise up and as long as we remind ourselves of what we have been and of what we shall become, as long as we remind ourselves of the promises of God, that very presence will be an accusation at the door of the South African government. It will be an unmasking act; it will be an exposure of what they are.

Since then we have heard of children of three years and five years and six years old, brutally murdered. Since then we have heard of Bernard Fortuin and others like him who had to die on the streets of Cape Town and elsewhere. Since then we have seen the children of Crossroads. We have seen incredible criminal acts played out right in front of our eyes.

We cannot forget because we are the Church. We are the body of Jesus Christ. And as long as these things happen, we know that the body of Christ is being broken every single day. As long as these things happen, Christ is again persecuted, denied and crucified. We are the Church and we are called to preach the Gospel of Jesus Christ, a Gospel of hope and liberation, but also a Gospel of judgement. And we must not be afraid to do that. We are the Church and we are called in this world to recognize the reality of evil. We are called to recognize the presence of the devil in the midst of our history.

Evil is real. We must not make the mistake of thinking that Satan is merely a figment of someone's imagination, or that Satan is no more than some nightclub comedian – usually painted with two little horns, usually black, usually with a long tail sticking out from somewhere. And we smile because we sophisticated people of the modern world cannot believe in that any more. I am telling you, please don't make that mistake, for Satan is alive. Satan is real. Satan is what he has always been – an adversary. He is the enemy of God and of God's people. He is a destroyer of peace and of all that is good. He is a liar and a deceiver. He is an accuser of God's children. That is what the Bible calls him, and the Bible speaks in graphic terms about the reality of evil and about the presence of Satan among God's people.

Satan is real. He does not and cannot abide love and peace and justice. He elevates propaganda and lies to the level of truth. He is real, and you see him on television trying to explain what the state of emergency means and why it is necessary. Satan is real, and from now on he will be the only one making press statements and explaining what has happened to people, because the press will not be allowed to be there. Satan is real, and he is alive and he has decided that he will let loose his roaring lions. They are out to devour all that they can find and no one will be able to say, "This is what has happened," because he has decided who will speak on whose behalf. And these independent witnesses that you see in front of you will not be allowed to show to the world what Satan is doing. He is doing it, but no one must know. And so all the people in Britain and in Europe and in the United

States who hear will not hear what is really happening, but only what he has decided that they will hear.

Satan is real and sometimes he is in the pulpit justifying the oppression of our people, telling our people – our people – that their oppression is somehow the will of God and there is nothing that we can do about it. When you are oppressed, don't worry about it: it's God's will. And when you are thrown in jail, don't worry about it: it's God's will. And when they take away your homes, don't worry about it: it's God's will. And when they detain you with your children, it's God's will; and when they burn down your shacks in Crossroads, it's God's will; and when they kill you on the streets, it's God's will. Satan is in the pulpit telling people that sometimes.

But we know that this is a lie. It is not God's will that our people should live the way we do. It is not God's will that we should have a government that understands nothing about justice and truth and freedom and dignity and humanity. It is not God's will that we suffer so. It is not God's will that Crossroads is what it is today. It is not God's will that a mother with a four-month-old baby and a six-year-old handicapped boy should be burned down in a shack while people stand by in their uniforms and do nothing about it. It is not God's will. God's will is for justice and for peace and for freedom and for dignity and for love and for genuine reconciliation.

Satan is real. Right now he has an order that says he can go around killing our people on the streets, and then he stands up in parliament justifying the murderers of our children. Don't you try to deceive yourself by acting as if he was not real. Recognize him for what he is. Know what we are dealing with at this stage of South Africa's history. We have arrived at one of the most difficult moments in our history. Already we are standing knee-deep in blood. The South African government is no longer a servant of God, but the beast from the sea, seeking whom it can devour. Our people are pushed relentlessly into more and more and more violence. We can see it, and we can no longer speak simply of a peaceful solution to our problems – not when our people are dying, when we are dying.

You know how our efforts for nonviolent change have all ended in massacres over the years: 1960 in Sharpeville, 1976 in Soweto, 1980 in Cape Town, and from 1983 onward. In 1985 we called together a march, a non violent peaceful march, simply to give a message to Nelson Mandela and to the world that he and others should be free, and that South Africa should begin to understand the realities of our situation. We did not have a single gun; we did not intend to look for one. We did not have a single stone; we did not intend to throw even one. And yet while I was in Pretoria maximum security prison and you went to the stadium for your peaceful demonstration, they came with their tear gas and their dogs and their guns and their bullets.

And still this is not enough. Our people are sometimes on the brink of despair. What else should we do? How else shall we show our protest? How else shall we give embodiment to our hope? How else shall we continue our struggle when all peaceful protests have been made impossible by this government, which then turns around and, with unbelievable hypocrisy, says that other people must first denounce violence so that we can all talk together?

In the meantime Britain and the United States continue to be the main supporters of this South African government. They continue to find excuses for this government. There is not enough reason, Britain says, to act. And the United States can only say that all sides must show restraint. For God's sake, Mr Reagan, what restraint must we show more than we have shown? Who are the people today, on this 16th June, who are walking around with guns and rifles and live ammunition? Who are the people who did so ten years ago? Who are the people who have done so consistently almost every day for the last ten years? What restraint must we show? How many white people have died at our hands, Mr Reagan? During the last ten years, how many white children have we shot, have we killed, have we locked up, have we tortured? What restraint are you talking about, Mr Reagan? I cannot begin to understand this hypocrisy. We are unarmed people. The restraint Mr Reagan is asking of us is not to restrain from violence, but to restrain and refrain from protesting. He wants us to accept this evil that is being done to our people. If this is what you ask, Mr President of the United States, please go and ask it elsewhere. We cannot give that to you.

Ronald Reagan and Margaret Thatcher know this: if the situation were reversed today, if Nelson Mandela were sitting in Pretoria and P. W. Botha in Robben Island, if white children were massacred on the street as black children are today, Ronald Reagan and Margaret Thatcher would have acted a long time ago. They would not have waited. Ronald Reagan knows he would have sent in his troops under some excuse, and he would have helped white South Africa in such a battle.

But it is because we are not white, my people, that this is happening. It is because your children's lives do not count in the eyes of Mr Reagan and Mrs Thatcher. I never thought that the day would come when I would have to say this from a public pulpit, but I am saying it now. Maybe there is nothing we can do about the United States of America, and maybe there is no way we can speak to the hearts of the people of Britain, but there is one thing that they must know. We are a people – weak as we are in terms of their understanding of power, weak as we are in terms of their military might and the military might of their friends in Pretoria – we are a people determined to be free. And there is nothing that they can do that will ever break the spirit of our people. There is nothing that they can do that will turn this tide of resistance. There is nothing that they can do that will turn us away from our goal. We have kept our feet on this course and we will walk it. We have seen the goal ahead and we will reach it. There is a fire that we have lit in our heart and it burns for freedom. It will not go out, and they must understand that.

I do not know what to say to you any more. For years now you have listened to me from pulpits and platforms, and you have heard me plead for our nonviolent resistance because I believe that that is the best way. That is the way of peace. You have heeded those calls, and you have come unarmed when we have called; we have participated in those actions, and you have responded, – and you today bear the scars of that action. So no one today in South Africa can simply call for nonviolent response. And yet I must plead with you. Somehow we must remember that the dream of God is one of peace and humanity. War and hatred and destruction is not God's will. I can no longer simply judge people who choose the path of violence, but I must say to you, Beware of what we do when we do it not merely for the sake of our just cause, but out of our anger and despair. I know I can no longer demand; I am simply asking and pleading in the midst of a situation that has already become too much for us to bear.

Let us also remember what Jesus says: "I have seen Satan fall like lightning from heaven." He does not say that he hopes to see Satan fall. He does not say, "I think Satan will fall". He does not say, "I will call together a commission of inquiry and they will look into the possibility of Satan's falling." He says, "I have seen Satan fall." That means that the power of Satan has already been broken. There are people who think that the declaration of a state of emergency is a sign of power on the part of the South African government. It is not. It is a sign of blind panic. It is a sign of desperation. It is a sign of their powerlessness. Violence is never a sign of power. Violence and hatred are never signs of how strong you are. It shows unashamedly the weaknesses of the oppressor. They have nothing else *but* violence. They have nothing else *but* theft. They have nothing else *but* murder and more senseless murder.

The state president in his speech the other day said a lot of things that we cannot go into now, but one thing he said that I cannot simply ignore is this. He said, "South Africa is quite alone now in the world", or something to that effect. "We only have", he says, "our forces to help us and our God." Now, he may have his forces to help him; that I will grant him. South Africa may be producing more guns than ever before; that I will grant him. They may have flown forty thousand more troops into Cape Town; that I will grant him. They may have powerful friends in the West; that I will grant him.

But what I cannot grant him is his bland assertion that they have God. Mr President, let me tell you clearly: the God you are talking about is not the God of the Bible. Woe to you, South African government, for your god is an idol! Your god is racism. Your god is·

oppression. Your god is guns and dogs and bullets. Your god has to be carried because he cannot walk. He has ears but he cannot hear. He has hands but he cannot help you. And in the end you will sit with all your gods surrounding you and you will be destroyed. Woe to you, South African government, for your life will end like the life of Pharaoh! Your life will end like the life of Ahab. Your life will end like the life of Jezebel. It is not I that says so; it is the Bible that says so.

So if you want to throw us in jail, do so. But don't think that you are doing it in the name of God who is the Father of Jesus Christ. If you want to destroy our communities, do so. But don't do it in the name of the God who is the Father of Jesus Christ. If you want to torture us in your prisons, do so. But don't think you can do it in the name of God who is the God of liberation and the God of Israel and the God of His people. If you want to kill us, do so. But don't think that you can do that in the name of the God of the Bible, for that God will rise up and that God will judge you for what you are. And that God will exact from you His just wage. That God will destroy all evil, including the evil of this government. Of that I am sure.

For Jesus has said, "I have seen Satan fall", Satan may be riding high today; Jesus says, "I have seen Satan fall", Satan may be getting his guns ready today; Jesus says, "I have seen Satan fall". And even as the troops converge upon us, I have seen Satan fall. And even as you glibly lie on your television and tell the world what is not happening, and take your lies and make them into truth, I have seen Satan fall. Even as the tears will again blind the eyes of all our mothers, I have seen Satan fall. And even though these prison doors shut behind us a hundred times, I have seen

Satan fall. And even as our blood continues to flow, I have seen Satan fall.

Do not despair. This is not the final chapter. For them yes, but not for us. Do not despair. Their guns will not have the last word. Do not despair. We are marching on to victory, and they know it. That is why they are doing what they are doing. Do not give up now. Let not fear overcome your hearts. Let not despair drive you into the wilderness of desperation. Do not turn your back now on the graves of our ıchildren. Fight on. Believe on. Struggle on. The moment is dark now, but the sun shall surely rise. The night is upon us, but the stars will not go out completely. Our dreams are within our hearts and almost within our grasp. Do not turn away now.

Believe the words of Jesus as you watch their television.

Believe the words of Jesus as you see their trucks patrolling our streets.

Believe the words of Jesus as you see the soldiers carrying their guns.

Believe the words of Jesus even as they detain you.

Believe the words of Jesus even as they scare you to death and kill you.

Believe the words of Jesus: **I have seen Satan fall. I have seen Satan fall. I have seen Satan fall. GOD BLESS YOU ALL!**

Fount Paperbacks

Fount is one of the leading paperback publishers of religious books and below are some of its recent titles.

- [ ] GETHSEMANE Martin Israel £2.50
- [ ] HIS HEALING TOUCH Michael Buckley £2.50
- [ ] YES TO LIFE David Clarke £2.95
- [ ] THE DIVORCED CATHOLIC Edmund Flood £1.95
- [ ] THE WORLD WALKS BY Sue Masham £2.95
- [ ] C. S. LEWIS: THE MAN AND HIS GOD
      Richard Harries £1.75
- [ ] BEING FRIENDS Peter Levin £2.95
- [ ] DON'T BE AFRAID TO SAY YOU'RE LONELY
      Christopher Martin £2.50
- [ ] BASIL HUME: A PORTRAIT Tony Castle (ed.) £3.50
- [ ] TERRY WAITE: MAN WITH A MISSION
      Trevor Barnes £2.95
- [ ] PRAYING THROUGH PARADOX Charles Elliott £2.50
- [ ] TIMELESS AT HEART C. S. Lewis £2.50
- [ ] THE POLITICS OF PARADISE Frank Field £3.50
- [ ] THE WOUNDED CITY Trevor Barnes £2.50
- [ ] THE SACRAMENT OF THE WORD Donald Coggan £2.95
- [ ] IS THERE ANYONE THERE? Richard MacKenna £1.95

All Fount paperbacks are available through your bookshop or newsagent, or they can be ordered by post from Fount Paperbacks, Cash Sales Department, G.P.O. Box 29, Douglas, Isle of Man. Please send purchase price plus 22p per book, maximum postage £3. Customers outside the UK send purchase price, plus 22p per book. Cheque, postal order or money order. No currency.

NAME (Block letters)_____

ADDRESS _____

_____

_____